Focus on WRITING 5

Laura Walsh

John Beaumont, Series Editor
Borough of Manhattan Community College
City University of New York

Focus on Writing 5

Pearson Education, 221 River Street, Hoboken, NJ 07030

Staff Credits: The people who made up the *Focus on Writing 5* team, representing editorial, production, design, and manufacturing, are Pietro Alongi, Rhea Banker, Danielle Belfiore, Elizabeth Carlson, Nan Clarke, Aerin Csigay, Dave Dickey, Christine Edmonds, Oliva Fernandez, Barry Katzen, Penny Laporte, Jaime Lieber, Tara Maceyak, Amy McCormick, Barbara Perez, Joan Poole, Debbie Sistino, Jane Townsend, and Adina Zoltan.

The Grammar Presentation charts in *Focus on Writing 5* are adapted from *Focus on Grammar 5, Fifth Edition*, by Jay Maurer, Pearson Education, Hoboken, New Jersey, © 2017.

Cover image: © Li Jingwang / Getty Images
Text composition: ElectraGraphics, Inc.
World map: Mapping Specialists, Limited

Library of Congress Cataloging-in-Publication Data
Haugnes, Natasha, 1965–
 Focus on writing. 1 / Natasha Haugnes.
   p. cm.
 Includes index.
 ISBN 0-13-231350-2 — ISBN 0-13-231352-9 — ISBN 0-13-231353-7 — ISBN 0-13-231354-5 — ISBN 0-13-231355-3 1. English language—Textbooks for foreign speakers. 2. English language—Rhetoric—Problems, exercises, etc. 3. Report writing—Problems, exercises, etc. I. Title.
 PE1128.H3934 2011
 428.2—dc22

                                                                    2011014764

PEARSON ELT ON THE **WEB**

Pearsonelt.com offers online resources for teachers and students. Acess our Companion Websites, our online catalog, and our local offices around the world.

Visit us at **pearsonelt.com.**

Printed in the United States of America

ISBN 10: 0-13-231355-3
ISBN 13: 978-0-13-231355-1

33 2020

Contents

To the Teacher

Focus on Writing is a five-level series that prepares students for academic coursework. Each book in the series gives students an essential set of tools to ensure that they master not only the writing process, but also the grammatical structures, lexical knowledge, and rhetorical modes required for academic writing. The series provides an incremental course of instruction that progresses from basic sentences (Book 1) and paragraphs (Books 1–3) to essays (Books 3–5). Grammar presentation and focused grammar practice are correlated to *Focus on Grammar*.

A Process Approach to Writing

Over the past 30 years, the *writing process* approach has become the primary paradigm for teaching writing. As cognitive research shows, writing is a recursive process. When students practice the entire writing process repeatedly with careful guidance, they internalize the essential steps, thereby improving their writing and their confidence in themselves as writers.

Each unit in each book of *Focus on Writing* provides direct instruction, clear examples, and continual practice in the writing process. Students draw on their prior knowledge, set goals, gather information, organize ideas and evidence, and monitor their own writing process. Students write topic-related sentences and use them in a basic paragraph (Book 1); they focus on writing an *introduction*, *body*, and *conclusion* for a paragraph (Books 2–3) or essay (Books 3–5). Whether students are writing a group of related sentences, a paragraph, or an essay, they produce a complete, cohesive piece of writing in *every* unit.

Predictable Step-by-Step Units

Focus on Writing is easy to use. Its predictable and consistent unit format guides students step by step through the writing process.

■ PLANNING FOR WRITING

Students are introduced to the unit theme through an engaging image and high-interest reading. Brainstorming tasks develop critical thinking and serve as a springboard for the unit's writing assignment. Vocabulary building activities and writing tips related to the topic and organizational focus of the unit provide opportunities for students to expand their own writing.

■ STEP 1: PREWRITING

In Book 1, students learn the basics of sentence structure and are encouraged to combine sentences into cohesive paragraphs. They choose between two authentic academic writing assignments, explore their ideas through discussions with classmates, and complete a graphic organizer.

In Books 2–5, students learn the basics of a rhetorical structure (e.g., narration, description, opinion, persuasion, compare-contrast, cause-effect or problem-solution) and choose between two authentic academic writing assignments. Students explore their ideas through freewriting, share them with classmates, and complete a graphic organizer.

STEP 2: WRITING THE FIRST DRAFT

Explanations, examples, and focused practice help students to prepare for their own writing assignment. Writing tasks guide students through the steps of the writing process as they analyze and develop topic sentences, body sentences, and concluding sentences (Books 1–3) and continue on to draft thesis statements and complete introductions, body paragraphs, and conclusions (Books 3–5). At all levels, students learn how to use transitions and other connecting words to knit the parts of their writing together.

STEP 3: REVISING

Before students revise their drafts, they read and analyze a writing model, complete vocabulary exercises, and review writing tips that they then apply to their own writing. A Revision Checklist tailored to the specific assignment guides students through the revision process.

STEP 4: EDITING

Grammar presentation and practice help students make the connection between grammar and writing. An Editing Checklist ensures students check and proofread their final drafts before giving them to their instructors.

Helpful Writing Tools

Each book in the series provides students with an array of writing tools to help them gain confidence in their writing skills.

- *Tip for Writers* presents a level-specific writing skill to help students with their assignment. The tips include asking *wh-* questions, using conjunctions to connect ideas, identifying audience, using descriptive details, and using pronoun referents.

- *Building Word Knowledge* sections give students explicit instruction in key vocabulary topics, for example, word families, collocations, compound nouns, and phrasal verbs.

- *Graphic organizers* help students generate and organize information for their writing assignment. For example, in Book 1, they fill out a timeline for a narrative paragraph and in Book 3, they complete a Venn diagram for a compare-contrast essay. In the final unit of Books 4 and 5, they use multiple organizers.

- *Sample paragraphs* and *essays* throughout the units, tied to the unit theme and writing assignments, provide clear models for students as they learn how to compose a topic sentence, thesis statement, introduction, body, and conclusion.

Carefully Targeted Grammar Instruction

Each unit in *Focus on Writing* helps students make the essential link between grammar and writing. The grammar topics for each unit are carefully chosen and correlated to *Focus on Grammar* to help students fulfill the writing goals of the unit.

Online Teacher's Manuals

The online Teacher's Manuals include model lesson plans, specific unit overviews, timed writing assignments, authentic student models for each assignment, rubrics targeted specifically for the writing assignment, and answer keys.

To the Student

Welcome to *Focus on Writing*! This book will help you develop your writing skills. You will learn about and practice the steps in the writing process.

All of the units are easy to follow. They include many examples, models, and, of course, lots of writing activities.

Read the explanations on the next few pages before you begin Unit 1.

> Before you begin to write, you need to know what you will write about. To help you, you will see the **writing focus** under the title of the unit. A picture, a short reading and a **brainstorming** activity will help you get ideas about a topic. Putting your ideas into a **graphic organizer** will help you structure your ideas.

UNIT 5 Problems in Sports

IN THIS UNIT You will be writing an essay about a problem in sports and a possible solution.

Athletes used to win competitions on the basis of skill, training, and teamwork, but now some athletes are taking drugs that can improve their performance. Even though most of these performance-enhancing drugs can cause serious health problems and are illegal, athletes continue to use them. What do you think should be done about the problem of athletes' drug use?

Planning for Writing

■ BRAINSTORM

A. Some sports in which athletes have been caught using performance-enhancing drugs are bicycle racing, Olympic running, and bodybuilding. Why do you think performance-enhancing drugs are illegal in sports? Discuss your answer with a partner.

B. Using a *Wh*- Questions Chart. You can use a *wh*- questions chart to gather information for a writing assignment.

Work with a partner. What information do you need in order to learn more about the problem of athletes' drug use? Make a list of questions to ask when you investigate.

Who?
What?
When?
Where?
Why? *Why do some athletes take illegal performance-enhancing drugs?*
How?

C. With your partner, brainstorm three possible solutions to the problem of drugs in sports.

1. _____
2. _____
3. _____

127

A **reading** about the topic will help you develop more ideas. The reading can be a newspaper or magazine article, a webpage, or a blog.

Building Word Knowledge activities introduce a vocabulary or dictionary skill that you will be able to use when you write your assignment. For example, you will practice using different word forms and collocations.

A useful **Tip for Writers** gives you specific writing tools, for example, how to use descriptive details and when to use conjunctions to connect ideas.

■ **READ**

Read the article about performance-enhancing drugs from an online South African magazine.

Athletes and drugs: an abusive relationship

By VRINDA MAHESHWARI in the *Daily Maverick*, 14 October 2010

1   The 2010 Commonwealth Games is just the latest sporting event tainted[1] by a doping scandal. Three athletes have tested positive for drugs so far, not counting athletes who tested positive before the Games even began. When will they ever learn? Will they ever learn?

2   The third positive drug test at the Commonwealth Games occurred on Wednesday. Rani Yadav, an Indian athlete who participated in the women's 20-kilometer (12.4 mile) walk, tested positive for a banned anabolic steroid[2] commonly called nandrolone. The Commonwealth Games Federation court has suspended Yadav until a hearing of the evidence. Use of nandrolone is prohibited by the World Anti-Doping Agency. The provisional suspension has come as a huge disappointment to the host country.

3   Lalit Bhanot, the secretary general of the organizing committee, called the latest incident "unfortunate." He said that the National Anti-Doping Agency had done its best to test athletes, but it was difficult to control doping if sportspeople were dedicated to taking banned substances. Doping has become a recurrent[3] problem in Indian sports, with weightlifting bearing the greatest load: The agency banned six offenders last year and almost as many so far this year. Three swimmers, six wrestlers, and one weightlifter from India have tested positive for the drug methylhexaneaemine in 2010 alone.

4   Of course, drugs and sports have gone hand-in-hand[4] since competitive events began. In ancient Greece, Olympic athletes would eat specially prepared meat (including lizards) and drink magic potions to boost their performances. Whether this actually worked or not is debatable, but there's no denying the intention to cheat was there.

5   It's no different in modern sport, which is rife with[5] suspicions about performance-enhancing drug use by many top athletes. The usual suspects are human-growth hormones (which promote physical development), anabolic steroids (drugs that resemble testosterone and control the metabolic rate), beta-blockers, erythropoietin, stimulants, and diuretics.

[1] **tainted:** affected by something dishonest
[2] **anabolic steroids:** drugs that make muscles grow quickly
[3] **recurrent:** repeated
[4] **hand-in-hand:** closely related or happening together
[5] **rife with:** full of something bad

Building Word Knowledge

Using Verb + Preposition and Adjective + Preposition Combinations. Many English verbs and adjectives are followed by prepositional phrases. It is important to learn the correct prepositions to put after the verbs and adjectives. Here are some examples of verb + preposition and adjective + preposition combinations from "Athletes and drugs: an abusive relationship."

Examples:

. . . who participated in the women's 20-kilometer walk

. . . if sportspeople were dedicated to taking banned substances

. . . Armstrong submitted to 24 unannounced drug tests

. . . he was disqualified for doping

Find five more verb + preposition or adjective + preposition combinations in the article on pages 128–129. Sometimes other words come between the verb or adjective and the preposition. Write the verbs or adjectives and the prepositions that follow them.

1. _____

2. _____

3. _____

4. _____

5. _____

Focused Practice

A. *Read the Tip for Writers. Find evidence in the article on pages 128–129 that supports the following claims. The first one is done for you.*

1. Doping has become a recurrent problem in Indian sports.

    The agency banned six offenders last year and almost as
    many so far this year. Three swimmers, six wrestlers, and
    one weightlifter from India have tested positive for the
    drug methylhexaneaemine in 2010 alone.

2. Drugs and sports have gone hand-in-hand since competitive events began.

    _____

    _____

    _____

    _____

3. The drugs pose genuine health risks.

    _____

    _____

    _____

    _____

> **Tip for Writers**
>
> When writers describe a problem, they need to **provide enough evidence** to convince the reader that the problem exists and is serious.

◼ STEP 1: PREWRITING

This section helps you further develop your ideas. It gives you a short explanation of the writing assignment. A small outline gives you a "picture" of the parts of the writing process.

The **Your Own Writing** section gives you a choice of two writing assignments. After you choose one of the assignments, you can begin to think about what you will write and share your ideas with a partner (**Checking in**). Finally, you will complete a **graphic organizer** with ideas for your own writing assignment.

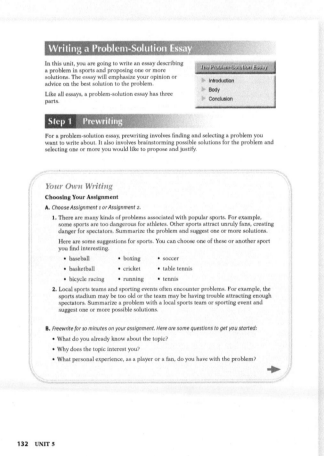

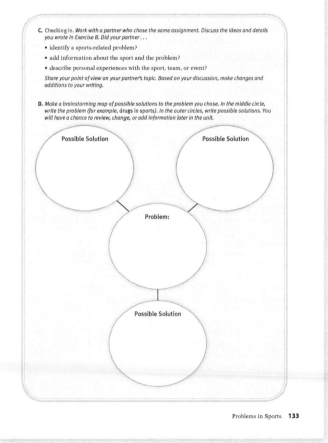

■ STEP 2: WRITING THE FIRST DRAFT

This section guides you through each part of your writing assignment. For a paragraph assignment, you will learn how to write a topic sentence, body sentences, and concluding sentence(s). For an essay assignment, you will learn how to write a thesis statement, introductory paragraph, body paragraph, and conclusion. At the end of Step 2, you will be able to write a complete first draft.

> **Focused Practice** activities will give you lots of writing practice *before* you draft your writing assignment. Make sure to look at all of the examples and models before you complete the exercises. The outline of the parts of the writing assignment helps you to keep track of where you are in the process.

Step 2 | Writing the First Draft

■ THE INTRODUCTION

In Unit 1, you learned that the introductory paragraph in an essay gives important background information to help the reader understand the thesis statement.

In a problem-solution essay, the introduction usually provides background information about the subject and introduces the problem. The thesis statement briefly states the problem and solution(s). It may be one or two sentences.

The Problem-Solution Essay

▼ Introduction
- Background Information
- Thesis Statement
  - Statement of the Problem
  - Possible Solution(s)

▶ Body

▶ Conclusion

Focused Practice

A. *Read the following essay assignment. Then decide which information you might use as background information for an introductory paragraph on the topic. Check (✓) the sentences you choose and discuss your choices with a partner.*

- *Ask yourself this question to help you: Is this information important?*
- *Give reasons for your choices when you and your partner have different opinions.*

Performance-enhancing drugs have become a big problem in sporting events all over the world. Summarize the problem and suggest one or more solutions.

_____ **1.** The most common drugs used in weightlifting are corticosteroids.

_____ **2.** Performance-enhancing drugs have ruined the careers of several world-famous athletes.

_____ **3.** Both the Olympics and the Commonwealth games have been affected by drugs.

_____ **4.** My favorite athlete would never take performance-enhancing drugs.

_____ **5.** Performance-enhancing drugs should be legal.

_____ **6.** Serious penalties for athletes have not solved the problem.

B. *Reread the essay assignment in Exercise A. Then, for the following thesis statement, decide which ideas will probably be developed in the essay. Check (✓) the sentences you choose and discuss your choices with a partner.*

Thesis Statement: Performance-enhancing drugs can unfairly advantage some athletes and seriously damage their health, so young people and adult athletes need to be educated about the dangers of these substances.

_____ **1.** Many athletes begin using drugs such as steroids at a young age.

_____ **2.** Different sporting events have different penalties for drug use.

_____ **3.** It is useless to ban drugs since athletes use them anyway.

_____ **4.** In some sports such as weightlifting, bodybuilding drugs have become part of the culture.

_____ **5.** Anabolic steroids can damage the liver.

_____ **6.** Marijuana is accepted as a medicine in some parts of the world.

C. *Read the introduction for an essay on the assignment in Exercise A (page 134). Then discuss the questions with a partner.*

> International sporting events provide an opportunity for athletes from around the world to compete in a healthy environment, away from the usual stress of international relations. Events such as the Olympics and the Commonwealth games are popular because the citizens of each country can cheer for their teams in fair contests. However, not all athletes follow the rules; some of them secretly take drugs. These drugs have ruined the careers of several talented athletes, who have disappointed their fans and fellow citizens. Performance-enhancing drugs can unfairly advantage some athletes and seriously damage their health, so young people and adult athletes need to be educated about the dangers of these substances.

1. Which ideas from Exercise A did the writer use as background?

2. Why did the writer omit some ideas but not others?

3. What is the writer's thesis statement? Underline it. Is it one sentence or two?

4. What problem and solution do you expect the essay to cover?

5. Why does the writer begin with two positive statements about the value of international sporting events?

■ STEP 3: REVISING

After you write your first draft, you aren't finished yet! Step 3 shows you how important it is to look again at your writing.

> Review and analyze the **model** paragraphs or essays to get an idea of what a well-written paragraph or essay looks like. You will see how the parts of your own writing should fit together.
>
> Completing the **Revision Checklists** for each writing assignment will help you identify parts of your draft that need improvement.

Step 3	Revising

Revising your work is an essential part of the writing process. This is your opportunity to be sure that your essay has all the important pieces and that it is clear.

Focused Practice

A. You have read parts of this problem-solution essay. Now read the entire essay to see how the parts fit together.

Ending the Drug Problem in Sports

International sporting events provide an opportunity for athletes from around the world to compete in a healthy environment, away from the usual stress of international relations. Events such as the Olympics and the Commonwealth games are popular because the citizens of each country can cheer for their teams in fair contests. However, not all athletes follow the rules; some of them secretly take drugs. These drugs have ruined the careers of several talented athletes, who have disappointed their fans and fellow citizens. Performance-enhancing drugs can unfairly advantage some athletes and seriously damage their health, so young people and adult athletes need to be educated about the dangers of these substances.

According to Vrinda Maheshwari in "Athletes and drugs: an abusive relationship," the use of performance-enhancing drugs in international sporting events has become a big problem for which there is no clear solution. The drug allegations at the 2010 Commonwealth Games have led Maheshwari to wonder if the athletes will ever stop using drugs. A spokesperson for the Commonwealth Games said that regular drug-testing by the National Anti-Doping Agency has not ended the problem. Athletes have always tried to boost their performance, and modern drugs have created an atmosphere of suspicion in sports. The most common performance-boosting drugs are human-growth hormones, anabolic steroids, beta-blockers, erythropoietin, stimulants, and diuretics. In addition to providing an unfair advantage to those who use them, these drugs also can damage the health of the athletes and have even caused death. Although some agencies are printing lists of banned substances and athletes suffer severe penalties when caught, so far no solutions to this problem have proved effective.

---

3. The continued use of performance-enhancing drugs will lead to more suspicion and disappointment for athletes and fans.

_____

_____

4. Athletes who want to attract fans should find fair and legal ways to prepare for competitions.

_____

_____

Your Own Writing

Revising Your Draft

A. Reread the first draft of your essay. Use the Revision Checklist to identify parts of your writing that might need improvement.

B. Review your plans and notes, and your responses to the Revision Checklist. Then revise your first draft. Save your revised essay. You will look at it again in the next section.

Revision Checklist

Did you . . .

☐ state the problem and proposed solution(s) in your thesis statement?

☐ provide enough background information in your introduction?

☐ summarize an article about a problem in sports in your first body paragraph?

☐ propose one or more solutions to the problem in your remaining body paragraphs?

☐ provide enough reasons and evidence to support your solution(s)?

☐ connect the parts of your essay with effective transition words and strategies?

☐ restate the problem and solution(s) in your conclusion?

☐ use an effective concluding strategy?

☐ use correct verb + preposition and adjective + preposition combinations?

☐ give your essay a good title?

☐ cite sources you used in your essay?

STEP 4: EDITING

In the final step, you review a grammar topic that will help you edit your revised draft. Then you use an Editing Checklist to correct your own paragraph or essay for any errors in grammar, punctuation, or spelling.

> **Grammar Presentation** charts present notes and examples on specific grammar topics related to your writing assignment. Then you follow up with grammar practice.
>
> **Editing Checklists** for each writing assignment help you correct and polish your final draft.

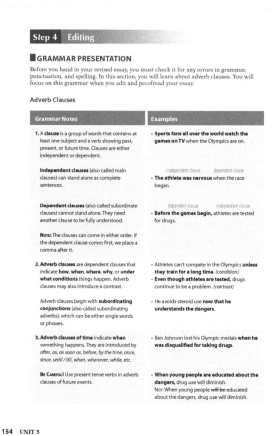

Step 4 Editing

GRAMMAR PRESENTATION

Before you hand in your revised essay, you must check it for any errors in grammar, punctuation, and spelling. In this section, you will learn about adverb clauses. You will focus on this grammar when you edit and proofread your essay.

Adverb Clauses

Grammar Notes	Examples
1. A **clause** is a group of words that contains at least one subject and a verb showing past, present, or future time. Clauses are either independent or dependent.	• **Sports fans all over the world watch the games on TV** when the Olympics are on.
Independent clauses (also called main clauses) can stand alone as complete sentences.	independent clause dependent clause • **The athlete was nervous** when the race began.
Dependent clauses (also called subordinate clauses) cannot stand alone. They need another clause to be fully understood. **Note:** The clauses can come in either order. If the dependent clause comes first, we place a comma after it.	dependent clause independent clause • **Before the games begin,** athletes are tested for drugs.
2. **Adverb clauses** are dependent clauses that indicate **how, when, where, why,** or **under what conditions** things happen. Adverb clauses may also introduce a contrast. Adverb clauses begin with **subordinating conjunctions** (also called subordinating adverbs), which can be either single words or phrases.	• Athletes can't compete in the Olympics **unless they train for a long time.** *(condition)* • **Even though athletes are tested,** drugs continue to be a problem. *(contrast)* • He avoids steroid use **now that he understands the dangers.**
3. **Adverb clauses of time** indicate **when** something happens. They are introduced by *after, as, as soon as, before, by the time, once, since, until / till, when, whenever, while,* etc. **Be Careful!** Use present tense verbs in adverb clauses of future events.	• Ben Johnson lost his Olympic medals **when he was disqualified for taking drugs.** • **When young people are educated about the dangers,** drug use will diminish. Not: When young people ~~will be~~ educated about the dangers, drug use will diminish.

---

paid athletes continue to play sports. Because the rewards make it all worthwhile. If we will continue to punish athletes for taking performance-enhancing drugs, we will waste time and lose many great athletes.

D. *Write five sentences related to the assignment you chose on page 132. Use adverb clauses. These may be sentences you already have in your essay.*

1. _____
   _____

2. _____
   _____

3. _____
   _____

4. _____
   _____

5. _____
   _____

Your Own Writing

Editing Your Draft

A. *Use the Editing Checklist to edit and proofread your essay.*

B. *Prepare a clean copy of the final draft of your essay and hand it in to your teacher.*

Editing Checklist
Did you . . .
☐ include adverb clauses and use them correctly?
☐ use correct verb forms, punctuation, and spelling?
☐ use verb + preposition and adjective + preposition combinations and other words correctly?

Now, you are ready to begin with Unit 1. Enjoy the writing process!

Scope and Sequence

UNIT	STEP 1 Planning and Prewriting	STEP 2 Writing the First Draft
1 Going Green *Writing Focus* Writing an essay *Reading* *The Green Travel Guide*, an excerpt from a book about ecotourism	Using a T-chart Using collocations Identifying the audience Choosing a writing assignment for an essay on the environment Freewriting about the topic Sharing points of view	Opening with an interesting fact Providing background information for an essay Writing thesis statements Researching, taking notes, and citing sources Writing topic sentences Clarifying transitions between ideas Including examples, facts, and figures Restating the thesis and using concluding strategies
2 New Media *Writing Focus* Writing a persuasive essay *Reading* *How to save journalism: can a government-subsidized press save democracy?* an article about old and new media	Using a T-chart Using phrasal verbs Identifying the purpose Choosing a writing assignment for a persuasive essay Freewriting about the topic Sharing points of view Researching, taking notes, and citing sources	Opening with a thoughtful question Providing background information for a persuasive essay Writing thesis statements that argue a claim Researching, taking notes, and citing sources Writing topic sentences Presenting the opposing point of view Developing and supporting a point of view Paraphrasing others' ideas Restating the thesis and using persuasive concluding strategies
3 Types of Intelligence *Writing Focus* Writing a compare-contrast essay *Reading* *Gardner's Theory of Multiple Intelligences*, excerpts from an IQ test and a psychology textbook	Using a Venn diagram Using word families Providing an explanation or example Choosing a writing assignment for a compare-contrast essay Freewriting about two subjects Sharing ideas and details about the two subjects	Identifying the purpose of the comparison Providing background information for a compare-contrast essay Writing thesis statements that give points of comparison and a purpose for the comparison Researching, taking notes, and citing sources Using the point-by-point or block method Signaling similarities and differences with compare-contrast words and expressions Restating the thesis and presenting the significance of the comparison

STEP 3 Revising	STEP 4 Editing	Learning Outcome	*Focus on Grammar Level 5, Fifth Edition*
Analyzing a model essay Writing sentences with collocations Applying the Revision Checklist and writing the second draft	Reviewing present, past, and future time Incorporating the grammar in sentences Editing a paragraph for grammatical correctness Applying the Editing Checklist and writing the final draft	Can evaluate different ideas or solutions to a problem. Can write clear, detailed essays in an assured, personal, natural style targeted to a specific audience.	**Unit 1** Present Time **Unit 2** Past Time **Unit 3** Future Time
Analyzing a model persuasive essay Using phrasal verbs correctly in sentences Applying the Revision Checklist and writing the second draft	Reviewing noun clauses: indirect speech Incorporating the grammar in sentences and conversations Editing a paragraph for grammatical correctness Applying the Editing Checklist and writing the final draft	Can write essays that develop an argument systematically with appropriate highlighting of significant points and relevant supporting detail.	**Unit 21** Direct and Indirect Speech
Analyzing a model compare-contrast essay Using correct word forms in sentences Applying the Revision Checklist and writing the second draft	Reviewing adjective clauses Incorporating the grammar in sentences and paragraphs Applying the Editing Checklist and writing the final draft	Can write clear, well-structured essays on complex subjects. Can expand and support points of view at some length with subsidiary points, reasons, and relevant examples. Can wrap up with an appropriate conclusion.	**Unit 14** Adjective Clauses **Unit 15** Adjective Clauses and Phrases

UNIT	STEP 1 Planning and Prewriting	STEP 2 Writing the First Draft
4 Crime *Writing Focus* Writing a cause-effect essay *Reading* *Identity fraud nightmare: One man's story*, an article about the crime of identity theft	Using a brainstorming map Using collocations Making time and cause-effect relationships clear Choosing a writing assignment for a cause-effect essay Freewriting about the topic Sharing points of view	Opening with an interesting example Providing background information for a cause-effect essay Writing thesis statements that focus on causes or effects Researching, taking notes, and citing sources Presenting evidence: facts, statistics, statements from authorities, examples, and personal stories Ordering paragraphs according to chronology, importance, or specificity Using words that express cause-effect relationships Restating the thesis and presenting the significance of the cause-effect analysis
5 Problems in Sports *Writing Focus* Writing a problem-solution essay *Reading* *Athletes and drugs: an abusive relationship*, an article about performance-enhancing drugs	Using a *wh-* questions chart Using verb + adjective and adjective + preposition combinations Providing enough evidence Choosing a writing assignment for a problem-solution essay Freewriting about the topic Using a brainstorming map Sharing points of view	Writing thesis statements that state problems and hint at solutions Providing background information for a problem-solution essay Researching, taking notes, and citing sources Writing topic sentences Summarizing information and writing a summary paragraph Using transition words and other techniques to connect paragraphs Restating the problem and solution(s) and using a concluding strategy
6 Communities *Writing Focus* Writing an essay with two or more structures *Reading* *Not Your Mother's Retirement Community*, an article about active retirement communities	Using a T-chart, Venn diagram, and brainstorming map Understanding and using figurative language Adopting an appropriate tone Choosing a writing assignment for an essay with multiple structures Freewriting about the topic Sharing points of view on the topic	Opening with a quotation Providing background information Writing thesis statements that express opinions Researching, taking notes, and citing sources Using words and phrases to signal a particular rhetorical structure Using quotations as support for the controlling ideas Restating the thesis and using a concluding strategy (such as looking to the future or presenting the opposing point of view)

STEP 3 Revising	STEP 4 Editing	Learning Outcome	*Focus on Grammar Level 5, Fifth Edition*
Analyzing a model cause-effect essay Completing a dialogue with collocations Applying the Revision Checklist and writing the second draft	Reviewing the passive voice Incorporating the grammar in sentences Editing a paragraph for grammatical correctness Applying the Editing Checklist and writing the final draft	Can write essays that develop an argument, giving reasons in support of or against a particular point of view. Can explain the advantages and disadvantages of various options. Can synthesize information and arguments from a number of sources.	**Unit 6** Passives: Part 1 **Unit 7** Passives: Part 2
Analyzing a model problem-solution essay Writing sentences with verb + preposition and adjective + preposition combinations Applying the Revision Checklist and writing the second draft	Reviewing adverb clauses Incorporating the grammar in sentences Editing a paragraph for grammatical correctness Applying the Editing Checklist and writing the final draft	Can evaluate different ideas or solutions to a problem. Can write an essay that conveys information and ideas on abstract as well as concrete topics. Can check information and explain problems with reasonable precision.	**Unit 17** Adverb Clauses
Analyzing a model essay with two or more structures Using figurative language in sentences Applying the Revision Checklist and writing the second draft	Reviewing the subjunctive Incorporating the grammar in sentences Editing a paragraph for grammatical correctness Applying the Editing Checklist and writing the final draft	Can produce clear, smoothly flowing, complex essays that present a case. Can provide an appropriate and effective logical structure that helps the reader to find significant points.	**Unit 23** More Conditions; The Subjunctive

UNIT 1 Going Green

IN THIS UNIT   You will be writing an essay about our relationship with the natural environment, in our role as consumers.

We all affect the environment where we live and also where we travel. Some tourist destinations are being damaged by the many people who visit them each year and by the surrounding development that takes place to attract visitors. Each year, more than 800,000 people visit Machu Picchu in Peru to marvel at the 500-year-old structures that were built from blocks of granite in the mountainside. The number of visitors has more than doubled since 2002, and it continues to grow. If you visit a historic site like this one, how can you take care of the environment?

Planning for Writing

■ BRAINSTORM

A. *Look at the photos of popular tourist destinations. Decide which one you would most like to visit. What would you like to see and do there? Discuss your choice with a partner.*

Pyramids in Egypt

The Great Wall of China

Italian village

Beach in Thailand

B. **Using a T-chart.** When you organize ideas on a topic, you can use a T-chart like the one below.

Work with a partner. Make a list of the problems that large numbers of visitors to the tourist destinations above might cause. If you know of problems in other tourist destinations, you can add them. Share your T-chart with the class.

Tourist Destination	Possible Problems
Ancient Egyptian pyramids and tombs	Excessive contact with tourists each year adds to the erosion of some ancient structures and artifacts.

READ

Read the excerpt from the book The Green Travel Guide.

THE GREEN TRAVEL GUIDE

1 What does increased travel and tourism mean for our environment? The unfortunate answer is quite a bit of harm. Of course, new developments in technology and resource management can help reduce the impact on the environment of our fondness for travel. We can build more efficient jet engines, use solar power to generate electricity, install toilets that use less water, and encourage off-season tourism. Even so, the toll of unregulated tourism and travel is a serious one:

2 • An estimated 70 percent of international travel trips are for pleasure. This can mean a vast expenditure of energy, and a colossal[1] amount of transport-generated pollution. According to one estimate, air travel alone is responsible for at least 5–6 percent of the global warming caused by the emission of greenhouse gas pollution, and it is expected to increase. Together, aircraft and cars, two of our favorite means of travel when we go on holiday, are carrying a large part of the responsibility for the pollution that a majority of scientists now believe is causing change in the Earth's climate patterns. Car exhaust pollution is also a major source of the smog-causing gases and chemical particulates[2] that doctors have linked with respiratory and other diseases.

3 • Tourism—even the so-called eco-tourism of nature-watching—can put pressure on some of the world's most fragile natural environments. In Snowdonia, the Lake District and the Peak District in Great Britain,[3] the tramping[4] feet of tens of thousands of hikers each year has caused serious erosion to some mountain paths. In the Galapagos Islands, off the Pacific coast of Ecuador, conservationists have persuaded the Ecuadorian authorities to begin limiting the number of tourists admitted each year. The conservationists fear that the associated pollution, added to the sheer numbers of visitors tramping across the islands, could be a threat to the existence of rare species, such as the marine iguanas, giant tortoises and various bird species found there. Tourist litter, such as discarded plastic bags and bottles, kills unwary wildlife around the world. In Greece and some other Mediterranean countries, the building of tourist hotels and discos has disrupted turtles nesting on nearby beaches.

4 • Unregulated, excess tourism can harm the man-made environment of historic towns and cities. Some Italian cities are now taking measures to limit the numbers of tourist buses allowed into their centers, fearing that the noise, exhaust emissions, and vibrations would damage ancient buildings.

5 • Large numbers of tourists can hurt local cultures and economies. In East Africa, Maasai tribal people were moved from some of their traditional areas to create room for new national parks, which have become a key attraction for tourists wanting to see the region's famous wildlife. In Kenya and in Goa,[5] water sources traditionally used by local people have been diverted to supply newly built tourist hotels and lodges. In Thailand and the Philippines, tens of thousands of young girls, and some young boys too, have been caught up in the prostitution which initially sprang up to cater to American troops during the Vietnam War. The child prostitution is now part of a "sex tourism" industry, often controlled by criminal gangs. In more remote parts of the world, indigenous[6] peoples fear that even the development of nature or "eco-tourism" is part of a process that will threaten their lands and autonomy,[7] leaving them as mere exotic sights for the tourists. Even in western Europe, there have been

---

[1] **colossal:** extremely large
[2] **particulates:** very small separate pieces of a substance, especially a substance in the air that comes from car engines and can damage your health
[3] **Great Britain:** part of the United Kingdom
[4] **tramping:** walking with heavy steps
[5] **Goa:** a state in western India
[6] **indigenous:** people, customs, etc., that have always been in a place, before other people or customs arrived
[7] **autonomy:** freedom to govern an area

protests that tourism, while benefiting local economies, can get out of control. Some islanders in Majorca[8] have called for a limit to further tourist developments. They object to the new building, water shortages, and sale of large numbers of homes and farms on the island to foreign visitors. Now Majorca informs all visitors of its Responsible Tourism Campaign.

6 The damage tourism causes can form a bleak picture. But there are positive signs that the travel and tourism industry, helped by green groups, conservation organizations and governments, is improving its performance. The individual traveler can also make a difference. A well-known environmental slogan for the green traveler is, "Take only photographs, leave only footprints." Can we achieve this? And can we learn to leave even lighter footprints?

---

[8] **Majorca:** one of the Balearic Islands off the east coast of Spain

Building Word Knowledge

Using Collocations. To write well, choose words and phrases that express your meaning accurately and naturally. In English, certain words frequently appear together. These word partners are called *collocations*. Here are some examples of collocations from *The Green Travel Guide*.

solar power: energy generated by the sun

global warming: an increase in the Earth's temperature caused by human activities, such as burning coal, oil, and natural gas

greenhouse gas: carbon dioxide or methane, which trap the heat above the Earth

indigenous people: people native to an area

green groups: organizations that support the environment

Find the collocations in the reading on pages 4–5. Notice how they are used.

Focused Practice

A. *Read the* Tip for Writers. *Discuss with a partner who the intended audience for* The Green Travel Guide *is. Then, on your own, write one or two sentences telling who the intended audience is and how you know this.*

_____

_____

_____

_____

> **Tip for Writers**
>
> As you plan your essay, **identify your audience**. For most academic writing, your audience will be your classmates and instructor.

B. *Look at the world map on pages 192–193. Work with a partner to locate each place on the map. Then reread the article to find the environmental problem caused by tourists to each. The first one is done for you.*

1. Great Britain (United Kingdom): *erosion to mountain paths from too many hikers*

2. Galapagos Islands: _____

3. Greece: _____

4. Italy: _____

5. East Africa: _____

6. Kenya: _____

7. Goa (India): _____

8. Thailand: _____

9. Philippines: _____

10. Majorca (Baleiric Islands): _____

C. *Based on your answers to Exercise B, discuss these questions with your partner. Then share your answers with the class.*

1. Do the authors of *The Green Travel Guide* believe that we will be able to solve all these environmental problems caused by tourists? If so, which ones?

2. Do you think they are hopeful about the future of travel and tourism and its effects on our environment? Find evidence (statements that make you believe this to be true) in the text to support your answer.

3. Explain the slogan "Take only photographs; leave only footprints." How could travelers change their behavior in order to follow this advice?

D. *Which problem discussed in* **The Green Travel Guide** *do you consider the most serious or important? What can people do to help solve this problem? Write a brief paragraph to answer these questions.*

_____

_____

_____

_____

_____

_____

_____

_____

Writing an Essay

In this unit, you are going to write an essay about the environment. All essays contain certain basic elements that you will need to include.

An essay contains three parts: an introduction, a body, and a conclusion.

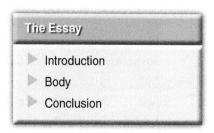

The Essay

▶ Introduction
▶ Body
▶ Conclusion

Step 1   Prewriting

Prewriting is an important step in the writing process. Here you choose what to write about and you begin to think of and jot down ideas. For an academic essay, the prewriting step involves planning your major points of discussion (your controlling ideas). It also includes brainstorming specific types of evidence to support your ideas.

Your Own Writing

Choosing Your Assignment

A. *Choose Assignment 1 or Assignment 2.*

   1. Considering all the environmental effects of producing and consuming petroleum products, should people continue to drive gasoline-powered vehicles? Why or why not?

   2. As consumers, we buy and use many different products each day. What should we do to avoid harming the world's environment and people?

B. *Freewrite for 10 minutes on your assignment. Here are some questions to get you started:*

   • What do you already know about the environmental effects of (Assignment 1) gasoline-powered vehicles or (Assignment 2) consumer products?

   • Why are these topics interesting to you?

   • What else do you want to find out about your topic?

C. Checking in. *Work with a partner who chose the same assignment. Discuss the ideas and details you wrote in Exercise B. Did your partner . . .*

   • write about the environmental effects of gasoline-powered vehicles or consumer products?

   • give suggestions on what consumers should do?

   Share your point of view on your partner's topic. Based on your discussion, make changes and additions to your writing.

D. *Complete the T-chart. Fill in the headings and as much information as you can. You will have a chance to review, change, or add information later in the unit.*

- If you chose Assignment 1, list benefits of gasoline-powered vehicles in the left column and the drawbacks in the right column.

- If you chose Assignment 2, list ways that consumers cause harm to the environment in the left column (problems). For example, consumers increase energy use through the purchase of food from distant lands. In the right column (ways to avoid problems), list ways that consumers could avoid causing these problems. For example, consumers could buy locally grown foods.

Step 2 Writing the First Draft

■ THE INTRODUCTION

The introductory paragraph in an essay contains three parts:

1. **An opening strategy** that attracts the interest of the reader. Many writers begin with an interesting or surprising fact.

2. **Background information** about the topic of the essay to help the reader understand and become interested in the topic. Before you begin, ask yourself, "What does the reader need to know about the topic? What information do I need to provide?" Do not give too many details. You will develop, or explain, your topic with more detailed information in the body of the essay.

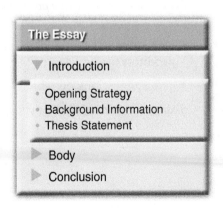

The Essay

▼ Introduction
- Opening Strategy
- Background Information
- Thesis Statement

▶ Body
▶ Conclusion

3. **A thesis statement** that presents the controlling (main) idea of the entire essay. It may be one or two sentences. The thesis statement responds directly to the assignment and presents an idea that will be developed in the essay. It may mention the author's purpose in writing as well as his or her point of view on the issue.

A successful thesis statement . . .

- presents the controlling idea of the entire essay.

- responds to the assignment.

- contains an idea that the writer will develop (explain) and support.

- does more than state a fact.

Example:

Essay Assignment: Considering all the negative effects of tourism on the environment, should people continue to travel to all parts of the world? Why or why not?

Thesis Statement: Even though these problems are serious, I believe that people who are careful to respect the environment should continue to travel because traveling offers many benefits to both the traveler and the destination region.

Focused Practice

A. *Read the following essay assignment. Then decide what kind of background information you might use for an introductory paragraph on the topic. Check (✔) the sentences you choose and discuss your choices with a partner.*

- Ask yourself this question to help you: *Is the information necessary?*

- Give reasons for your choices when you and your partner have different opinions.

Considering all the negative effects of tourism on the environment, should people continue to travel to all parts of the world? Why or why not?

_____ **1.** the number of international tourists every year

_____ **2.** the 10 most popular tourist destinations

_____ **3.** common problems caused by tourism

_____ **4.** one or two specific examples of the problems caused by tourism

_____ **5.** the size of automobile and jet engines

_____ **6.** one or two examples of the benefits of travel

_____ **7.** a scientific explanation of climate change (global warming)

B. *Read the introduction of an essay from the assignment in Exercise A (page 9). Then work with a partner to complete the chart below, using words from the introduction.*

> In 2009, 880 million people traveled to foreign countries as tourists enjoying their leisure time, and the number is expected to grow in the future. Most people travel to explore new regions, geography, wildlife, and cultures, and to learn more about the world. However, the number of tourists has begun to have negative effects on the land, animals, and people in popular tourist destinations. For example, increased tourism has endangered the lives of some rare species of animals and caused some indigenous people to lose their homes. Even though these problems are serious, I believe that people who are careful to respect the environment should continue to travel because traveling offers many benefits to both the traveler and the destination region.

Interesting Opening Fact	
Background Information from Exercise A	1. 2. 3. 4.
Writer's Point of View (Thesis Statement)	

C. *Reread the thesis statement at the end of the introductory paragraph in Exercise B. Discuss with a partner what makes it a good thesis statement.*

D. *Read the other possible thesis statements for the essay assignment in Exercise A. Then check (✓) the items that are true for each statement.*

1. **Thesis Statement:** Even though tourism has many negative effects, more people are traveling today than ever before.

   _____ **a.** Presents the controlling idea of the entire essay *(Could an entire essay be written on this?)*

   _____ **b.** Responds to the assignment

   _____ **c.** Contains an idea that the writer will develop and support

   _____ **d.** Does more than state a fact

2. **Thesis Statement:** I believe that people should stop traveling so much because there is no way to prevent all the negative effects of travel on the environment.

   _____ **a.** Presents the controlling idea of the entire essay *(Could an entire essay be written on this?)*

   _____ **b.** Responds to the assignment

   _____ **c.** Contains an idea that the writer will develop and support

   _____ **d.** Does more than state a fact

3. **Thesis Statement:** In my opinion, rich tourists are all selfish people.

   _____ **a.** Presents the controlling idea of the entire essay *(Could an entire essay be written on this?)*

   _____ **b.** Responds to the assignment

   _____ **c.** Contains an idea that the writer will develop and support

   _____ **d.** Does more than state a fact

4. **Thesis Statement:** I believe that tourists should continue to travel if they do everything possible to prevent the negative effects on people and the environment.

   _____ **a.** Presents the controlling idea of the entire essay *(Could an entire essay be written on this?)*

   _____ **b.** Responds to the assignment

   _____ **c.** Contains an idea that the writer will develop and support

   _____ **d.** Does more than state a fact

Your Own Writing

Finding Out More

A. *Learn more about the topic you chose for your essay. Review the guidelines for researching a topic in the Appendix on pages 194–195.*

B. *Research the topic online or at the library.*

- If you chose Assignment 1, find out more about the negative effects of producing and consuming petroleum products. Research the Gulf of Mexico oil spill in 2010 and other consequences of oil drilling and exploration. Find out more about alternatives to gasoline-powered vehicles. Look for answers to the question: *Are these alternatives safe, practical, affordable, available?* You may want to use the following keywords when you search for information online: *hybrid cars, alternative fuels.*

- If you chose Assignment 2, find out more about our consumption of food, clothing, and other material goods. Locate answers to questions such as these: *Where do most of our goods come from? What environmental problems are caused in the process?* You may want to use the following keywords when you search for information online: *environmental effects, electronic waste.*

C. *Take notes on what you found out. For example:*

- Record key information about the products and the environment.

- Note the complete sources for your information, including the author, publication, medium (e.g., print, Web, DVD), place of publication, date, and page number, if appropriate.

- Add relevant information about your topic to the T-chart on page 8.

Use this information when you write your essay.

D. Checking in. *Share your information with a partner. Did your partner . . .*

- gather enough facts and details about the environmental effects?

- use at least three reliable sources?

Planning Your Introduction

A. *Find a surprising fact to open your introduction and catch your reader's attention. Write a sentence that presents this fact.*

_____

_____

B. *List the background information you will need to include in your introduction.*

_____

_____

_____

C. *Write a draft of your thesis statement. Make sure your thesis statement answers the question in the assignment and clearly presents your point of view. Look back at your freewriting and T-chart to help you.*

_____

_____

D. **Checking in.** *Share your thesis statement with a partner. Does your partner's thesis statement . . .*

- present the controlling idea of the entire essay?
- respond to the assignment?
- contain an idea that your partner will develop and support?
- do more than state a fact?

Tell your partner what kind of supporting evidence you expect to see in his or her essay, based on the thesis statement. Based on your partner's feedback, you may want to rewrite your thesis statement.

■ THE BODY

The body of an essay consists of one or more paragraphs in which you present and develop ideas to support your thesis statement. It is important to develop, or explain, your ideas clearly and to support them with specific details, such as facts and examples, to convince your readers to share your opinion.

In this unit, you will be writing a persuasive essay with two or more body paragraphs that support your point of view on an environmental issue.

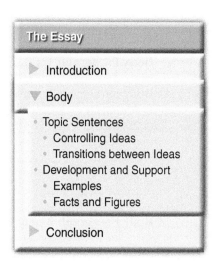

The Essay

- ▶ Introduction
- ▼ Body
  - Topic Sentences
    - Controlling Ideas
    - Transitions between Ideas
  - Development and Support
    - Examples
    - Facts and Figures
- ▶ Conclusion

Developing and Supporting the Thesis

One way to develop a thesis statement is to ask questions about the idea(s) it contains. If you look at the underlined ideas in the example thesis statement on page 14, you will notice that each idea needs to be developed and supported with specific details. The example shows you the type of questions you can ask to develop each underlined idea.

Example:

Thesis Statement: Even though these problems are serious, I believe that people who are careful to <u>respect the environment</u> should continue to travel because traveling offers <u>many benefits to both the traveler and the region</u>.

Idea 1: "respect the environment"

Ask yourself: _How can travelers respect the environment?_

    Body Paragraph 1: _ways for travelers to respect the environment_

Idea 2: "many benefits"

Ask yourself: _Who benefits from tourism? What are the benefits?_

    Body Paragraph 2: _benefits of tourism for the traveler_

    Body Paragraph 3: _benefits of tourism for the tourist destination_

Focused Practice

Write questions that would help develop the underlined ideas in the following thesis statements. Then plan body paragraphs to respond to the questions, as shown in the previous example.

1. **Thesis Statement:** International travel is not a good idea because it <u>causes too many environmental problems</u> and can be easily replaced by <u>modern media alternatives</u>.

   Idea 1: "causes too many environmental problems"

   Ask yourself: _____

   _____?

       Body Paragraph 1: _____

       Body Paragraph 2 (Optional): _____

   Idea 2: "modern media alternatives"

   Ask yourself: _____

   _____?

       Body Paragraph 2 or 3: _____

   _____

2. **Thesis Statement:** International travelers should stop visiting <u>countries where indigenous people and cultures are being harmed</u>.

   Idea 1: "countries where indigenous people and cultures are being harmed"

   Ask yourself: _____

   _____?

       Body Paragraph 1: _____

       Body Paragraph 2: _____

Writing Topic Sentences

Body paragraphs usually begin with a topic sentence. The topic sentence clearly states the controlling idea of the paragraph without using the same words as the thesis statement:

Example:

Thesis Statement: Even though these problems are serious, I believe that people who are careful to respect the environment should continue to travel because traveling offers many benefits to both the traveler and the destination region.

Topic Sentence for Body Paragraph 1: There are many ways for "green travelers" to avoid harming the environment.

In the body paragraphs that follow, the topic sentence often provides a transition from the idea in the previous body paragraph:

Example:

Topic Sentence for Body Paragraph 2: People who are careful not to damage the environment in these important ways can still enjoy important benefits from travel.

In this case, the topic sentence

- provides a transition from the previous paragraph:

  ↑ People who are careful not to damage the environment in these important ways . . .

- and also states the controlling idea of Body Paragraph 2:

  . . . can still enjoy important benefits from travel. ↓

Sometimes an entire sentence can provide a transition from the previous body paragraph:

Example:

Beginning of Body Paragraph 3: It is not only the traveler who benefits from the transaction. In many cases, the destination city or region enjoys benefits too.

In this case,

- the first sentence provides a transition from Body Paragraph 2:

  ↑ It is not only the traveler who benefits from the transaction.

- and the second sentence states the controlling idea of Body Paragraph 3:

  In many cases, the destination city or region enjoys benefits too. ↓

Focused Practice

A. *Read each topic sentence taken from a student essay. Circle the part of the sentence that connects with the thesis statement or the previous body paragraph, and underline the part of the sentence that states the controlling idea of the paragraph. The first sentence is done for you.*

1. Another reason to avoid travel is the global warming caused by airplanes.

2. Tourists can also cause problems for the indigenous people who live in these remote areas of the earth.

3. The most important benefit of travel is the opportunity to observe other cultures and ways of life.

(continued)

4. Given these obvious advantages of travel, why do I still plan to stay at home?

5. Face-to-face contact is not the only way to see the wonders of the world; photographic images of most places are available in books, in movies, and, most conveniently, on the Internet.

B. *Write a topic sentence for each body paragraph. Make sure the topic sentence for the second paragraph provides a transition from the first paragraph.*

1. _____

_____

Tourists often demand modern hotels and restaurants in areas where the infrastructure is not in place to support them. Many people want to visit African wildlife refuges, but what happens to the natural habitat when so much of the land is covered with hotels, swimming pools, and coffee shops? Even more destructive are the airports that are springing up in the last great wilderness areas on Earth. Some thoughtless tourists even leave behind mountains of trash from the disposable products that they bring with them.

2. _____

_____

Exhaust from automobiles and tourist buses can affect ancient sites over time. Egypt has had to restrict road access to the famous pyramids and tombs. Roads that carry tourists often damage, or place too much strain on, the natural landscape. For example, the delicate ecosystems in the African grasslands suffer damage from the crisscrossing safari roads. More importantly, the exhaust from the cars and planes that carry tourists adds to the greenhouse gasses that cause global warming.

Developing a Body Paragraph

It is important to fully develop and support the controlling idea of each body paragraph. In this book, you will learn and practice several ways to develop a paragraph. In this unit, you will practice developing two important types of supporting evidence (details):

- **Examples:** Most body paragraphs in an academic essay contain multiple examples because it usually takes more than one example to support a point. Examples may be one or more sentences.

- **Facts and Figures:** An interesting paragraph must be more than a list of facts and figures. However, factual material that is appropriately used is one of the strongest kinds of evidence that a writer can include.

Focused Practice

A. *Read the following body paragraph from* **The Green Travel Guide.** *Then work with a partner to list the examples it contains. The first one is done for you.*

Large numbers of tourists can hurt local cultures and economies. In East Africa, Maasai tribal people were moved from some of their traditional areas to create room for new national parks, which have become a key attraction for tourists wanting to see the region's famous wildlife. In Kenya and in Goa, water sources traditionally used by local people have been diverted to supply newly built tourist hotels and lodges. In Thailand and the Philippines, tens of thousands of young girls, and some young boys too, have been caught up in the prostitution which initially sprang up to cater to American troops during the Vietnam War. The child prostitution is now part of a "sex tourism" industry, often controlled by criminal gangs. In more remote parts of the world, indigenous peoples fear that even the development of nature or "eco-tourism" is part of a process that will threaten their lands and autonomy, leaving them as mere exotic sights for the tourists. Even in western Europe, there have been protests that tourism, while benefiting local economies, can get out of control. Some islanders in Majorca have called for a limit to further tourist developments. They object to the new building, water shortages, and sale of large numbers of homes and farms on the island to foreign visitors. Now Majorca informs all visitors of its Responsible Tourism Campaign.

Topic Sentence: Large numbers of tourists can hurt local cultures and economies.

Example 1: _The Maasai tribal people were moved._

Example 2: _____

Example 3: _____

Example 4: _____

Example 5: _____

B. *Review your answers to Exercise A. Check (✓) any of the examples you found that were explained in more than one sentence.*

C. *Read the following paragraph from* **The Green Travel Guide.** *Then with a partner underline the facts and figures it contains. The first one is done for you.*

> An estimated 70 percent of international travel trips are for pleasure. This can mean a vast expenditure of energy, and a colossal amount of transport-generated pollution. According to one estimate, air travel alone is responsible for at least 5-6 percent of the global warming caused by the emission of greenhouse gas pollution, and it is expected to increase. Together, aircraft and cars, two of our favorite means of travel when we go on holiday, are carrying a large part of the responsibility for the pollution that a majority of scientists now believe is causing change in the Earth's climate patterns. Car exhaust pollution is also a major source of the smog-causing gases and chemical particulates doctors have linked with respiratory and other diseases.

D. *Work with a partner to complete the plan for a paragraph with multiple examples. Share your plan with the class.*

Body Paragraph 1

Topic Sentence: There are many ways for "green travelers" to avoid harming the environment.

Example 1: _____

Example 2: _____

Example 3: _____

Example 4: _____

Your Own Writing

Planning Your Body Paragraphs

A. *Review your thesis statement and ask yourself these questions.*

1. Which ideas in this statement need to be explained or supported in my essay?

2. How many body paragraphs will this explanation require?

3. What will the controlling idea of each body paragraph be?

B. *Before you begin writing your body paragraphs, complete the outline. Copy your thesis statement from page 13.*

Essay

▷ Thesis Statement: _____

_____

▷ Body Paragraph 1

  ▷ Topic Sentence: _____

  _____

    ▷ Supporting Details (examples, facts, and figures):

      • _____

      • _____

      • _____

▷ Body Paragraph 2

  ▷ Topic Sentence: _____

  _____

    ▷ Supporting Details:

      • _____

      • _____

      • _____

▷ Body Paragraph 3 (Optional)

  ▷ Topic Sentence: _____

  _____

    ▷ Supporting Details:

      • _____

      • _____

      • _____

- provide interesting examples or facts?

- add enough facts and figures?

Based on your partner's feedback, you may want to rewrite parts of your outline.

■ THE CONCLUSION

The conclusion is where you return to the idea in the thesis statement in order to leave the reader with a strong impression and a clear idea about the topic. Writers usually restate the thesis in different words. In a persuasive essay about the environment, you might first summarize all the reasons why your plan for consumers is a good idea and then restate your plan.

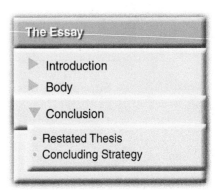

The Essay

▶ Introduction
▶ Body
▼ Conclusion
  • Restated Thesis
  • Concluding Strategy

Here are two strategies you might want to use to end your essay about the environment:

1. Look to the future of the environment and show how your idea will help make a positive difference.

2. Encourage readers to take action to help the environment, such as using public transportation or vehicles that use less (or no) gasoline.

Focused Practice

Read the following concluding paragraph and answer the questions.

> Even with all the photos and films in the world, there is no substitute for the personal experience of visiting an African wildlife park or the ancient ruins of Egypt or Rome, so those of us who are careful not to harm these amazing places should continue our journeys. But we shouldn't complain about the discomfort of local accommodations or restrictions on automobiles. After all, we are there to educate ourselves, not to bring noise or pollution. In the future, we will learn to see the world without harming its people or landscapes and enjoy the challenges.

1. What is the writer's restated thesis? Circle the sentence.

2. What concluding strategy does the writer use? Does the writer (1) look to the future or (2) encourage the reader to take action? Underline the sentence(s).

Your Own Writing

Planning Your Conclusion

A. *What will you put in your conclusion? List your ideas here.*

_____

_____

B. *Write the sentence that will remind the reader of your thesis statement.*

_____

_____

C. *What strategy will you use to close the essay?*

_____

_____

D. Checking in. *Share your ideas with a partner. Did your partner . . .*

- choose an effective strategy?

- return to the idea in the thesis statement in a new and interesting way?

Writing Your First Draft

A. *Read the* Tip for Writers. *Review your notes on pages 8, 12–13, and 19. Then write the first draft of your essay. When you are finished, give your essay a working title.*

Tip for Writers

When you write your first draft, be sure that you have a clearly defined audience in mind.

B. *After you write the first draft, put in citations for any sources of information that you used. Use MLA (Modern Language Association) style for citations within and at the end of your essay. (See Unit 2 pages 49–50 and the Appendix on pages 194–195 for more information on and examples of MLA format.)*

Examples:

In 2009, 880 million people traveled to foreign countries as tourists enjoying their leisure time, and the number is expected to grow in the future (World Tourism Organization).

Works Cited

Chelsea. "Economic Benefits of Ecotourism in South Africa." *tourismroi.com.* Tourism ROI, 28 May 2008. Web. 28 Jan. 2011.

"Travelers Offer Glimpse into Tripadvisor 2009 Trends." *Tripadvisor.com.* Tripadvisor.com, 9 Oct. 2008. Web. 28 Jan. 2011.

World Tourism Organization UNWTO. United Nations, 2010. Web. 28 Jan. 2011.

C. *Hand in your draft to your teacher.*

Revising your work is an essential part of the writing process. This is your opportunity to be sure that your essay has all the important pieces and that it is clear.

Focused Practice

A. *You have read parts of this essay. Now read the entire essay to see how the parts fit together.*

Greener Travelers

In 2009, 880 million people traveled to foreign countries as tourists enjoying their leisure time, and the number is expected to grow in the future (World Tourism Organization). Most people travel to explore new regions, geography, wildlife, and cultures, and to learn more about the world. However, the number of tourists has begun to have negative effects on the land, animals, and people in popular tourist destinations. For example, increased tourism has endangered the lives of some rare species of animals and caused some indigenous people to lose their homes. Even though these problems are serious, I believe that people who are careful to respect the environment should continue to travel because traveling offers many benefits to both the traveler and the destination region.

There are many ways for "green travelers" to avoid harming the environment. Many countries offer alternatives to air travel for short distances, so travelers can lower their contribution to global warming. In Japan and Europe, it is possible to go almost anywhere by train. Travelers can save energy and enjoy the scenery at the same time. Once they arrive, visitors can get around on buses or bicycles, or even try walking or hiking. Tourists can also choose accommodations that practice conservation. In 2009, 34 percent of U.S. respondents said they would visit an environmentally friendly hotel or resort in the coming year, up from 30 percent in 2008 ("Travelers Offer Glimpse"). Tourists need to be more responsible about other ways of preserving the landscape, such as picking up their own trash. Most importantly, visitors to foreign countries need to respect the indigenous people and their right to their ancestral land.

People who are careful not to damage the environment in these important ways can still enjoy many benefits from travel. After all, young people can learn as much from travel as they do from school and studying, especially in the summer when they need a break from the pressures of school. "Ecotourism" can be very educational. Last summer, when I visited my native country, Guatemala, I rode my bicycle around the countryside to visit markets and volunteer in food programs. Travel can also bring a family close together, providing wonderful memories for parents and children. Parents can take the opportunity to teach children about the lands and cultures of the places they visit.

It is not only the traveler who benefits from these actions. In many cases, the destination city or region enjoys benefits too. Tourism can benefit a region economically by providing money and employment. For example, Kruger National Park in South Africa had more than one million visitors in 2008 and provided 60,000 jobs for South Africans (Chelsea). Increases in tourism are often linked with better roads and conditions for local communities too.

Even with all the photos and films in the world, there is no substitute for the personal experience of visiting an African wildlife park or the ancient ruins of Egypt or Rome, so those of us who are careful not to harm these amazing places should continue our travels. But we shouldn't complain about the discomfort of local accommodations or restrictions on automobiles. After all, we are there to educate ourselves, not to bring noise or pollution. In the future, we will learn to see the world without harming its people or landscapes and enjoy the challenges.

Works Cited

Chelsea. "Economic Benefits of Ecotourism in South Africa." *tourismroi.com.*
    Tourism ROI. 28 May 2008. Web. 28 Jan. 2011.

"Travelers Offer Glimpse into Tripadvisor 2009 Trends." *Tripadvisor.com.*
    Tripadvisor.com, 9 Oct. 2008. Web. 28 Jan. 2011.

World Tourism Organization UNWTO. United Nations, 2010. Web. 28 Jan. 2011.

B. *Work with a partner to answer the questions about the essay.*

1. What interesting or surprising fact did the writer use to open the essay? Circle it.
2. What is the thesis statement? Underline it.
3. What parts of the thesis statement are developed in the body paragraphs? Double underline them.
4. What is the controlling idea of paragraph 2? Underline the sentence that states it.

(continued)

5. What is the controlling idea of paragraph 3? Underline the sentence that states it.

6. Which sentence in paragraph 4 provides a transition from the previous paragraph into paragraph 4? Circle it.

7. What is the controlling idea of paragraph 4? Underline the sentence that states it.

8. What details, such as facts, figures, and examples, support the controlling ideas in each body paragraph? Check (✓) three kinds of support in each paragraph.

9. Where does the writer call the reader to join him or her in positive action? Underline the sentence(s).

10. How many works were cited by the author? Circle the in-text citations and the list of works cited.

C. **Checking in.** *Discuss your marked-up essays with another pair of students. Then in your group, share what you found most interesting about the essay. Explain your answer.*

Building Word Knowledge

The writer included many travel-related collocations in "Greener Travelers," including *leisure time, indigenous people, global warming, native country,* and *ancient ruins*.

A. *Work with a partner. Use each word in the list to form two collocations. Notice that sometimes the word comes first and sometimes it comes second. The first set is done for you.*

environmentally	room	tourist	train	~~travel~~

1. _____*travel*_____ agent   green _____*travel*_____

2. hotel _____   _____ reservation

3. catch a _____   _____ station

4. _____ attraction   _____ destination

5. _____ friendly   _____ safe

B. *Write sentences for three of the collocations in Exercise A. Share your sentences with a partner.*

1. _____

   _____

2. _____

   _____

3. _____

   _____

Your Own Writing

Revising Your Draft

A. *Reread the first draft of your essay. Use the Revision Checklist to identify parts of your writing that might need improvement.*

B. *Review your plans and notes, and your responses to the Revision Checklist. Then revise your first draft. Save your revised essay. You will look at it again in the next section.*

Revision Checklist

Did you . . .

☐ keep your intended audience in mind as you wrote?

☐ open your essay with an interesting or surprising fact?

☐ express the controlling idea of the entire essay in your thesis statement?

☐ give enough background information in your introduction?

☐ develop ideas in your thesis statement in each of your body paragraphs?

☐ give enough supporting details, such as facts, figures, and examples, to support the controlling idea of each paragraph?

☐ use your topic sentences to connect the ideas in your body paragraphs?

☐ restate the controlling idea of the entire essay in your conclusion?

☐ use an effective concluding strategy?

☐ use any collocations in your essay?

☐ give your essay a good title?

■ GRAMMAR PRESENTATION

Before you hand in your revised essay, you must check it for any errors in grammar, punctuation, and spelling. In this section, you will learn about present, past, and future time. You will focus on this grammar when you edit and proofread your essay.

Present, Past, and Future Time

Grammar Notes	Examples
1. Use the **simple present** to show actions, events, or states that are true in general or happen habitually.	• Most people **travel** to learn more about the world. (*true in general*) • Every summer, my family **visits** my grandparents. (*habitual*)
Remember to add *-s* to third person singular verbs in the simple present.	• An experienced traveler **packs** a light suitcase.
2. Use the **present progressive** to show actions or events that are currently in progress (not finished).	• The number of tourists **is growing**.
BE CAREFUL! We generally don't use the progressive with non-action verbs.	• We **need** to pick up our own trash. NOT: We're needing to pick up our own trash.
3. The **present perfect** and the **present perfect progressive** connect the past and the present. Use them to show actions that began in the past and continue until now.	• Egypt **has had** a thriving tourist industry for centuries. • I **have been writing** a blog about ecotourism for five years. • Since 2008, Majorca **has been informing** tourists of its Responsible Tourism Campaign.
They are often used with *for* + a length of time and *since* + a starting point.	
Use the past participle form of regular and irregular verbs.	REGULAR: has informed IRREGULAR: has had
4. Use the **simple past** to express an action, event, or state completed at a general or specific time in the past.	• In 2008, Kruger National Park **provided** 60,000 jobs for South Africans. • Last summer, I **rode** my bicycle around Guatemala.
Use the past form of regular and irregular verbs.	REGULAR: provided IRREGULAR: rode

5. Use **will** or **be going to** to say what you think will happen in the future.

BE CAREFUL! Use *will*, not *be going to*, to express an unplanned future action.

NOTE: We most often use *be going to*, not *will*, to talk about a future situation that is planned or already developing.

• In the future, more countries **will offer** alternatives to air travel for short distances.

• Travel with me. I **will change** my plans. Not: I ~~am going~~ to change my plans.

• Thirty-four percent of Americans **are going to** search for an environmentally friendly hotel this year.

Focused Practice

A. *Use the simple present or present progressive in these sentences.*

1. My family can't afford an overseas vacation. It _____ too much.
(cost)

2. Some countries _____ measures to limit the numbers of tourists and
(now, take)
tour buses.

3. Car exhaust pollution _____ a major source of greenhouse gasses.
(be)

4. In general, I _____ with the authors of *The Green Travel Guide*.
(agree)

5. Many of my friends _____ to stay home and relax during
(love)
school vacations.

B. *Use the simple present, present perfect, or simple past in these sentences. For some sentences, more than one answer is possible.*

1. In the past two years, more than one million tourists _____
(visit)
Machu Picchu in Peru.

2. These days, most international trips _____ for pleasure.
(be)

3. Since ancient times, tourists _____ bringing home pieces of
(always, enjoy)
native artwork.

4. In a 2009 survey, 34 percent of Americans _____ that they would visit
(predict)
an environmentally friendly hotel in the coming year.

5. When I _____ a child, my family _____ short vacations
(be)   (take)
close to home.

C. *Use the simple present or future in these sentences. For some sentences, more than one answer is possible.*

1. More Americans _____ to take "green" vacations next year.
   (plan)

2. My family _____ the mountains near our hometown as soon as I
   (explore)
   return from school.

3. Every year thousands of international travelers _____ the Golden Gate
   (cross)
   Bridge in San Francisco.

4. I _____ at the airport at 5:00 P.M. tomorrow.
   (pick up, you)

5. Some indigenous people are afraid that tourism _____ their lands if
   (threaten)
   steps to limit it are not taken soon.

D. *Read and edit the following paragraph. There are eight mistakes in the use of verb forms. The first one is already corrected. Find and correct seven more.*

> *brings*
> Every year tourism ~~brought~~ many benefits to popular destinations around
> the world. The economic benefits to the local population are clear in business
> and employment. For example, in 2010, the tourist industry supplies Egypt with
> 2,543,000 jobs and provides nearly $11 billion of income to local businesses. And
> often the businesses serve the local population as well. In many countries, farmers'
> markets have begin to appear, which benefits visitors and local residents. The
> residents also benefitting from improvements to roads, housing, and airports. In
> fact, many public spaces and lands are maintained with tourist dollars. Tourists
> valued the preservation of the mountains, beaches, and cities that they have spend
> so much money to visit. In the future, ecotourism is bringing more improvements
> to the environment.

E. *Write five sentences related to the assignment you chose on page 7. Use different verb forms to show present, past, and future time as in the chart on pages 26–27. These may be sentences you already have in your essay.*

1. _____
   _____

2. _____
   _____

3. _____
   _____

4. _____
   _____

5. _____
   _____

Your Own Writing

Editing Your Draft

A. *Use the Editing Checklist to edit and proofread your essay.*

B. *Prepare a clean copy of the final draft of your essay and hand it in to your teacher.*

Editing Checklist
Did you . . .
☐ use the appropriate verb forms to show present, past, and future time?
☐ use correct punctuation and spelling?
☐ use collocations and other words correctly?

UNIT 2 New Media

IN THIS UNIT You will be writing a persuasive essay about the role of media in society and in our personal lives.

Old media, such as newspapers, radio, and television, are losing customers as more people, especially young people, get their news from new media, such as Internet news sites or blogs. Although the new media offer many advantages, some people do not believe that the new media can keep us well informed. Do you think that the new media offer more advantages or more disadvantages to readers, viewers, and listeners?

Planning for Writing

◼ BRAINSTORM

A. *For each category below, circle the source of news that you prefer or add a source of your own. Then discuss your choices in small groups.*

BEST SOURCE FOR

Sports News

Radio   Television   Newspaper   Internet   Other: _____

National News

Radio   Television   Newspaper   Internet   Other: _____

International News

Radio   Television   Newspaper   Internet   Other: _____

Local News

Radio   Television   Newspaper   Internet   Other: _____

Breaking News (as it happens)

Radio   Television   Newspaper   Internet   Other: _____

Entertainment News

Radio   Television   Newspaper   Internet   Other: _____

B. Using a T-chart. When you write about advantages and disadvantages, you can use a T-chart like the one below to organize your ideas.

Work with your group to make a list of the advantages and disadvantages of the new media as a source of news. Then share your list with the class.

Advantages	Disadvantages
Convenience: it's always available on my computer	

How to save journalism: can a government-subsidized press save democracy?

By Danny Duncan Collum

1   Thomas Jefferson, the third President of the United States, famously wrote that given a choice between a society with no newspapers and a society with no government, he would choose the latter. Well, the United States might be facing the former problem, and soon.

2   The news about newspapers just keeps getting worse. Since the subject was last broached[1] on this page just two months ago, the *Rocky Mountain News* in Denver has closed and the *Seattle Post-Intelligencer* has ceased print publication (both were second papers in two-paper towns). Detroit's papers, the *Free Press* and the *News*, have cut home delivery back to three print editions per week, and the owner of the *San Francisco Chronicle* is threatening to shut his paper down entirely. By the end of this year, there could be at least one important American city without a single daily newspaper.

3   One quick and easy response to the death of the newspaper is, "So what?" After all, there's a seemingly infinite array of news readily available, for free, on the Internet. But people who depend for news on Yahoo or Google, or even *The Huffington Post*, an online news magazine, need to stop and think. Where do the links on those sites lead you? Usually to the website of a daily newspaper. Where did bloggers first see the stories upon which they pass the day ruminating?[2] In a daily newspaper—or at least on a daily newspaper's website.

4   News reporters and writers have traditionally been free to write the truth, even if powerful forces like the government or big business don't approve. Daily newspapers still employ almost all the people who are, at least occasionally, doing the independent journalism that is essential to a free society. And these journalists can't just "move to the Web." The *Post-Intelligencer*, for instance, is continuing as a website with a staff of twenty journalists. The old print edition had a news staff of 165.

5   Lots of people are talking about this problem now, and in the April 6, 2009, issue of *The Nation*, journalist John Nichols and media professor Robert McChesney put forward the first modest proposal for what to do about it. When Nichols and McChesney speak, people interested in media reform listen. They were cofounders of *Free Press*, one of the most important vehicles in the media reform movement of recent years. The reformers staged a mass rebellion against Federal Communications Commission rulings on concentrated media ownership because they objected to the way that a few large companies own most American media outlets, such as newspapers and radio and television stations.

6   Nichols and McChesney's plan for saving American journalism calls for a significant investment of public resources. They want to maintain a journalistic infrastructure of media outlets that will guarantee every American's access to the information required for self-governance in a democratic society. In plain English, that means government subsidies[3] for the news media.

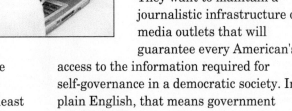

---

[1] **broached:** opened for discussion
[2] **ruminating:** thinking
[3] **subsidies:** financial support for someone or something that is producing goods or services

Building Word Knowledge

Using Phrasal Verbs. Some English verbs combine with a preposition or an adverb to form a meaning that is different from the verb alone. Phrasal verbs, as they are called, are common in informal conversation, but we often use them in written English too. The boldfaced phrasal verbs in the sentences below appear in "How to save journalism: Can a government-subsidized press save democracy?"

The newspapers have **cut** home delivery **back**.

The owner of the *San Francisco Chronicle* is threatening to **shut** his paper **down**.

Lots of people are **talking about** this problem.

A journalist and a professor **put forward** a modest proposal.

The plan **calls for** an investment of public resources.

Look at the phrasal verbs in the reading on page 32. Notice how they are used. For example, in separable phrasal verbs, a direct object can come between the two parts, as in cut *home delivery* back.

Focused Practice

A. *Read the* Tip for Writers. *With a partner, discuss the writer's main purpose for writing "How to save journalism: can a government-subsidized press save democracy?" Then on your own, write a sentence telling what the writer's purpose is and how you know this.*

_____

_____

_____

> ### Tip for Writers
>
> In a persuasive essay, your audience may not agree with you immediately (or ever), but will be open to considering your point of view. Before you begin writing, **identify the purpose** of your essay.

B. *Reread the article. Then work with a partner to choose the correct answers to the questions about its main ideas.*

1. According to the article, what is the bad news about newspapers?

    a. Newspapers are wasting too many trees for paper.

    b. Many newspapers are cutting back or going out of business.

    c. Newspaper reporters are quitting their jobs.

2. Where do websites such as Yahoo or Google get the news?

    a. newspapers or newspaper websites

    b. Yahoo blogs

    c. an infinite array of free news

3. What do John Nichols and Robert McChesney propose?

    a. an important vehicle for media reform

    b. government funding of the Internet

    c. government funding of old media

4. Why does the author of the article feel that independent journalism is important?

    a. Journalists depend too much on the government.

    b. A free society requires independent journalism for accurate information.

    c. Journalists can't just move to the Web.

C. *Read the statements. Decide with a partner whether each statement is true (T) or false (F) based on information in the article. Discuss the reasons for your answers and correct any false statements.*

_____ **1.** Thomas Jefferson thought newspapers were important.

_____ **2.** The *San Francisco Chronicle* ceased publication.

_____ **3.** Several important American cities have no daily newspapers.

_____ **4.** Almost all independent journalism is done by reporters for daily newspapers.

_____ **5.** Bloggers usually research and report their own stories.

_____ **6.** When it became a website, the *Post-Intelligencer* fired most of its reporters.

D. *Choose one of the following news sources. Write a paragraph explaining why you think it is a good source of news.*

| Internet | Newspaper | Radio | Television |

_____

_____

_____

_____

_____

_____

_____

_____

_____

Writing a Persuasive Essay

In this unit, you are going to write a persuasive academic essay. A persuasive essay gives a clear, strong point of view on a topic or question. When you attempt to persuade your reader to agree with your point of view, you often show the ways that opposing points of view are mistaken.

Like all essays, a persuasive essay has three parts.

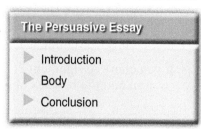

The Persuasive Essay

▶ Introduction
▶ Body
▶ Conclusion

Step 1 Prewriting

For a persuasive essay, prewriting involves selecting a topic you feel strongly about and clarifying your point of view about it. It also includes brainstorming ideas to establish specific points of support (evidence) for your point of view.

Your Own Writing

Choosing Your Assignment

A. *Choose Assignment 1 or Assignment 2.*

1. Social media, such as Facebook and Twitter, do not report the news. Instead, they provide opportunities to meet or stay connected with friends. Discuss the advantages or disadvantages of social media in our modern lives. Decide whether social media are beneficial or harmful. Support your point of view with reasons and examples.

2. Independent journalists investigate news stories and report the truth. In some countries, where the government controls the news media and the Internet, journalists are not independent. Do you believe that journalists should be free to report the truth as they see it, or do you believe that government control of the media is beneficial, especially in this Internet age? Support your point of view with reasons and examples.

B. *Freewrite for 10 minutes on your assignment. Here are some questions to get you started:*

- What do you already know about social media or government control of media?

- How has your personal experience shaped your point of view?

- What more do you want to find out about your topic?

C. **Checking in.** *Work with a partner who chose the same assignment. Discuss the ideas and details you wrote in Exercise B. Did your partner . . .*

- express a point of view on the issue?

- discuss the reasons for his or her point of view?

Share your point of view on your partner's topic. Based on your discussion, make changes and additions to your writing.

D. *Complete the T-chart. Fill in as much information as you can. You will have a chance to review, change, or add information later in the unit.*

- If you chose Assignment 1, list the advantages and disadvantages of social media.
- If you chose Assignment 2, list the benefits of independent journalism in the left column and the benefits of government-controlled media in the right column.

Step 2   Writing the First Draft

▮ THE INTRODUCTION

You learned in Unit 1 (pages 8–9) that the introductory paragraph in an essay gives important background information to help the reader understand the thesis statement.

In Unit 1, you practiced opening your essay with an interesting or surprising fact. Another opening strategy is to ask a thoughtful question.

In a persuasive essay, the thesis statement presents a claim that is *arguable*—that is, a claim that may be opposed by someone with a contrasting point of view. An academic argument may present a strong point of view, but it always contains reasonable and solid evidence to support it.

A successful thesis statement for a persuasive essay . . .

- presents the controlling idea of the entire essay.
- responds to the assignment.
- contains an idea that the writer will develop (explain) and support.
- does more than state a fact; usually presents an arguable assertion or claim.

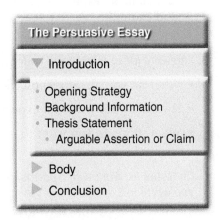

The Persuasive Essay

▼ Introduction
- Opening Strategy
- Background Information
- Thesis Statement
  - Arguable Assertion or Claim

▶ Body
▶ Conclusion

If you read the following examples, you will notice the difference between statements that can be argued and supported and those that cannot.

Examples:

1. I believe that reading newspapers is not very much fun.

In the first statement, the writer expresses a dislike—reading newspapers. This opinion is not arguable because it is based solely on the writer's personal preference.

2. Newspapers, television, and radio were the most important sources of news before the arrival of the Internet.

In the second statement, the writer expresses an obvious fact that hardly anyone would dispute. Therefore, it is not arguable.

3. The new media offer so many advantages over the traditional media that they could easily become better sources of news than any we have ever had.

In the third statement, the writer takes a definite stand on the new media and presents an arguable claim that he or she will need to support by explaining, in detail, the advantages of the new media as a source of news. The writer will also need to explain how the media will need to evolve to become even better.

Focused Practice

A. *Read the following essay assignment. Then decide what kind of background information you might use for an introductory paragraph on the topic. Check (✓) the sentences you choose and discuss your choices with a partner.*

- Ask yourself this question to help you: *Is this information necessary?*
- Give reasons for your choices when you and your partner have different opinions.

For generations, Americans have gotten their news from newspapers, radio, and television. This is now changing as more people turn to Internet sites for news stories and updates. Some even wonder if the traditional media are necessary in our society, with so much information available on the Internet. Discuss the advantages or disadvantages of the new media as a source of news. Support your point of view with reasons and examples.

_____ **1.** For many years, television has been the most popular source of news in America.

_____ **2.** Many American newspapers have been losing readers in the last few years.

_____ **3.** The Internet is becoming more popular as a source of news.

_____ **4.** Readers can comment on Internet news stories if they wish.

_____ **5.** Newspapers provide more information than do television or radio.

_____ **6.** Some people think that we no longer need newspapers, television, or radio news.

_____ **7.** Most people in North America now have Internet access.

_____ **8.** Some newspapers are going out of business.

_____ **9.** Young people prefer the Internet as a source of news.

B. *Read the introduction of an essay for the assignment in Exercise A (page 37). Then work with a partner to complete the chart below, using words from the introduction.*

> As the number of Internet users continues to grow, do you think that the Internet will change the way we read and think about the news? As more and more people, especially young people, turn to the Internet for news about world and local events, we find that newspapers, television, and radio news have been losing their audience or even going out of business. Some people are concerned about this shift because newspapers provide important in-depth coverage of events, while some Internet news sites only report opinions or repeat what is already in the newspapers. However, the new media offer so many advantages over the traditional media that they could easily become better sources of news than any we have ever had.

Thoughtful Question	
Background Information from Exercise A	1. 2. 3. 4. 5.
Writer's Point of View (Thesis Statement)	

C. *Reread the essay assignment in Exercise A (page 37). Then read the following thesis statements. Decide whether each sentence is a statement of fact (F), an unsupportable opinion (O), or an arguable claim (C). Explain your choices to a partner. The first one is done for you.*

__C__ **1.** The advantages of the new media are outweighed by several serious disadvantages.

_____ **2.** I love reading the news on the Internet.

_____ **3.** Newspapers, television, and radio are popular all over the world.

_____ **4.** The new media provide many important benefits to the reading audience.

_____ **5.** In my opinion, traditional print journalism will never disappear.

_____ **6.** I think that newspapers waste too many trees.

_____ **7.** If we examine the potential benefits of new media, it is clear that they can replace traditional media with no loss to society.

_____ **8.** The number of Internet users grows every year.

Your Own Writing

Finding Out More

A. *Learn more about the topic you chose for your essay. Research the topic online or at the library.*

- If you chose Assignment 1, find several articles about social media such as Facebook or Twitter. Gather information about the applications, the number of users, and the rate of growth. You may want to use the following keywords when you search for information online: *Facebook, Twitter, social media, social networks.*

  You may also want to survey and/or interview friends and classmates on their use of social media. Ask questions similar to the ones listed below.

  - What type of social media do you use, and why do you like them?

  - How many "friends" or "followers" do you have?

  - What problems have you had with social media?

  Keep track of the results for use in your essay. Record interesting things that your classmates say, and use these quotations in your essay. For any interviews, record the person's full name (correctly spelled) and the date.

- If you chose Assignment 2, find several articles about independent journalism. Locate answers to questions such as these: *Which countries support a free press? Which countries control the media?* You may want to use the following keywords when you search for information online: *free press, censorship.*

B. *Take notes on what you found out. For example:*

- Record key information about social or news media.

- Note the complete sources for your information including the author, title, publisher, place of publication, date, medium, and page number, if appropriate.

- Add relevant information to the T-chart on page 36.

Use this information when you write your essay.

C. Checking in. *Share your information with a partner. If your partner did a survey or series of interviews, did he or she . . .*

- record and count the responses to the survey?

- record names, dates, and quotations for the interviews?

If your partner found several articles, did he or she . . .

- find ones that relate to the assignment?

- record important information?

Planning Your Introduction

A. *Write a thoughtful question to attract your reader's attention.*

_____

_____

B. *List the background information you will need to include in your introduction.*

_____

_____

_____

C. *Write a draft of your thesis statement. Make sure your thesis statement answers the question in the assignment and clearly presents your point of view. Look back at your freewriting and T-chart to help you.*

_____

_____

D. Checking in. *Share your thesis statement with a partner. Does your partner's thesis statement . . .*

- present the controlling idea of the entire essay?
- respond to the assignment?
- contain an idea that your partner will develop and support?
- state more than a fact? Does it present an arguable assertion or claim?

Tell your partner what kind of supporting evidence you expect to see in his or her essay, based on the thesis statement. Based on your partner's feedback, you may want to rewrite your thesis statement.

■ THE BODY

In a persuasive essay, it is important to develop, or explain, your ideas clearly and to support them with evidence, such as specific facts and examples, to convince your readers to share your opinion. It is also important to maintain a reasonable tone and find common ground with those who oppose you. You need to anticipate and address their views. For example, if you write an essay in favor of the new media as sources of news, you need to anticipate some of the objections to the new media, such as inadequate reporting of the news.

If you write a separate body paragraph for the opposing point of view, you will need at least three body paragraphs in your essay. If you include a sentence or two from the opposing point of view in each body paragraph, you will need at least two body paragraphs. As in all essays, each body paragraph has a topic sentence, usually at or near the beginning of the paragraph.

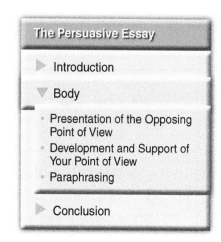

Presenting the Opposing Point of View in Body Paragraphs

As you know, a body paragraph supports the position you take in your thesis statement. However, both sides of a controversy may have good justifications for their positions. If you can anticipate the other side's arguments, you can counter them effectively. If you pretend that their arguments don't exist, you may weaken your own argument.

There are three ways that you can organize your essay to include the opposing point of view (or counterargument):

Examples:

Organization 1: Begin the body with a paragraph on the opposing point of view.

Body Paragraph 1: Opposing point of view (counterargument)

Body Paragraph 2: First reason/advantage/disadvantage for your point of view

Body Paragraph 3: Second reason/advantage/disadvantage for your point of view

Body Paragraph 4: Third reason/advantage/disadvantage for your point of view

Organization 2: End the body with a paragraph on the opposing point of view.

Body Paragraph 1: First reason/advantage/disadvantage for your point of view

Body Paragraph 2: Second reason/advantage/disadvantage for your point of view

Body Paragraph 3: Third reason/advantage/disadvantage for your point of view

Body Paragraph 4: Opposing point of view (counterargument)

Organization 3: Add the opposing point of view to each body paragraph when necessary.

Body Paragraph 1: First reason/advantage/disadvantage (and the opposing point of view)

Body Paragraph 2: Second reason/advantage/disadvantage (and the opposing point of view)

Body Paragraph 3: Third reason/advantage/disadvantage (and the opposing point of view)

Focused Practice

Read the following thesis statement and the body paragraph, which expresses the opposing point of view. Then work with a partner to answer the questions below.

> **Thesis Statement:** The new media offer so many advantages over the traditional media that they could easily become better sources of news than any we have ever had.
>
> We cannot deny that the traditional media have long served as excellent sources of news for societies around the world. Newspapers employ large staffs of reporters to investigate and report on politics, business, sports, entertainment, science, and the arts. Danny Duncan Collum, a writer for *Sojourners* magazine, claims that most independent investigative journalists in this country still work for daily newspapers. Newspapers are an important part of every community in a free society because readers trust them to challenge authority and report the truth. Television and radio news are popular and convenient ways to see and hear the latest news. The "seeing" on television is especially important. Videos of news events, such as violent crimes or wars, have a great deal of influence on public opinion. Many people feel that the traditional media simply cannot be replaced by the news available on computers and smart phones.

1. The topic sentence expresses the opposing point of view. Underline it.

2. Which words in the topic sentence signal that the opposite point of view is being expressed? Circle them.

3. Check (✓) each reason that is offered in support of the opposing point of view. How many reasons are there? _____

Developing Body Paragraphs

In a persuasive essay, it is especially important to carefully develop and support your ideas in order to convince your reader to accept your point of view. In Unit 1, you practiced two important forms of support:

- Examples
- Facts and Figures

In Unit 2, you will also practice supporting your ideas by using:

- **Reasoned Arguments:** Writers present logical reasons to support their arguments or to counter the arguments of the other side.

- **Statements from Authorities:** Writers provide the name and position of an authority on the subject.

Focused Practice

A. *Read the following model body paragraph. Then complete the chart.*

> In many other ways too, an important advantage of the new media is their interactivity. Most news stories are followed by comment sections on which readers can post their comments and respond to one another. Entries are often in the hundreds for major news. Sometimes the writer of the story responds to these comments with more information, turning the news report into an interactive community discussion. According to Claire Cain Miller of the *New York Times*, 25 percent of Internet news readers contribute to comment sections, and 80 percent email stories to their friends. Although some reader comments can be pointlessly argumentative and angry, most come from concerned citizens who wish to participate more fully in discussions of important news. The letters-to-the-editor section of traditional newspapers serves the same function but is not nearly as interactive. It is clear that better forums for citizen participation can only improve the quality of our government and our lives.

Topic Sentence

Reasoned Arguments   1.

2.

3.

Statement from Authority

B. *Work with a partner to add ideas of your own to the following paragraph chart. Then share your chart with the class.*

Topic Sentence	Television is the best medium for news.
Reasoned Arguments with Examples	1. Televisions and television broadcasting are available in most of the world at an affordable price. Example: Even in developing countries, most households own a television set. 2. Example: 3. Example:
Statement from Authority	
Facts and Statistics	1. Three quarters of Americans watch television news. 2.

Paraphrasing

When writers use statements from authorities or other writers, they often paraphrase the ideas, putting them into other words without changing the meaning. They also change the original language by using a different subject and verb or by altering, in some other way, the structure of the sentence. The following example shows the process of paraphrasing a sentence.

Example:

Original Sentence: Daily newspapers still employ almost all the people who are, at least occasionally, doing the independent "truth-to-power" journalism that is essential to a free society.

Paraphrase 1: Most of the investigative journalism in this country continues to be done by reporters for daily newspapers.

Paraphrase 2: Danny Duncan Collum, a writer for *Sojourners* magazine, claims that most independent investigative journalists in this country still work for daily newspapers.

Notice that paraphrase 2 has credited the author of the idea, making it a statement from an authority. This strengthens your own position in your essay.

Focused Practice

A. *Identify the subject and verb in each of the following sentences. Then write a paraphrase with a different sentence structure, using a different subject and verb. Be careful not to change the meaning of the sentence. The first one is done for you.*

1. "The owner of the *San Francisco Chronicle* is threatening to shut his paper down entirely."

   Subject: _____owner_____ Verb: _____shut down_____

   Paraphrase with different subject and verb:

   A major daily might go out of business. _____

2. "Lots of people are talking about this problem now."

   Subject: _____ Verb: _____

   Paraphrase with different subject and verb:

   _____

   _____

3. "There's a seemingly infinite array of news readily available, for free, on the Internet."

   Subject: _____ Verb: _____

   Paraphrase with different subject and verb:

   _____

   _____

4. "By the end of this year, there could be at least one important American city without a single daily newspaper."

   Subject: _____ Verb: _____

   Paraphrase with different subject and verb:

   _____

   _____

B. *Use one of the articles you found about the topic you chose on page 35. Choose two sentences to paraphrase and then decide if you want to use them in your essay.*

1. Sentence from source: _____

_____

Subject: _____ Verb: _____

Paraphrase with different subject and verb: _____

_____

2. Sentence from source: _____

_____

Subject: _____ Verb: _____

Paraphrase with different subject and verb: _____

_____

Your Own Writing

Planning Your Body Paragraphs

A. *Before you begin writing your body paragraphs, complete the following outline.*

- Copy your thesis statement from page 40.
- Organize your essay according to one of the three methods shown on page 41. Select the method and length that work best for your topic.
- If you want to experiment with more than one method of organization, complete additional outlines on a separate sheet of paper.

Persuasive Essay

▶ Thesis Statement: _____

_____

▶ Body Paragraph 1

  ▶ Topic Sentence: _____

  _____

    ▶ Supporting Details (reasoned arguments, examples, facts):

     • _____

     • _____

     • _____

▶ Body Paragraph 2

    ▶ Topic Sentence: _____

    _____

        ▶ Supporting Details:

          • _____

          • _____

          • _____

▶ Body Paragraph 3

    ▶ Topic Sentence: _____

    _____

        ▶ Supporting Details:

          • _____

          • _____

          • _____

▶ Body Paragraph 4

    ▶ Topic Sentence: _____

    _____

        ▶ Supporting Details:

          • _____

          • _____

          • _____

B. Checking in. *Share your outline with a partner. Did your partner . . .*

- choose the organization that works best for the essay?
- state the opposing point of view clearly?
- include interesting supporting evidence?

Based on your partner's feedback, you may want to rewrite parts of your outline.

■THE CONCLUSION

In the concluding paragraph of a persuasive essay, writers return to the controlling idea in the thesis statement in order to leave the reader with a clear sense of their point of view and perhaps a good reason to adopt the point of view. They usually restate the thesis in different words. In a persuasive essay about social media, for example, you might first summarize all the advantages or disadvantages of social media, and then make a recommendation for their appropriate use.

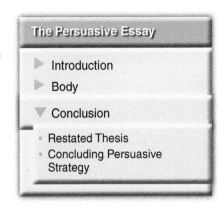

Here are four strategies you might want to use to end your essay about the media:

1. Summarize the opposing point of view that you described in your essay, and show once again why it is wrong.

2. Encourage the reader to agree with you. For example, ask the reader to take a survey of his or her friends and acquaintances to see if the results are different from yours.

3. Encourage the reader to take action. For example, encourage the reader to use social media in moderation.

4. Look to the future. For example, point out how your concluding advice will improve the future situation.

Focused Practice

Read the following concluding paragraph and answer the questions.

> It is clear that the new media advantages in convenience, interactivity, and interconnectivity create a rich environment for the news. As the reading public, we need to make sure that we don't lose the advantages of the old media, especially the tradition of independent daily newspapers. We need to know where our news is coming from. We should demand the best investigative journalism from the sites we use. We can't let newspapers die off while the Internet becomes a mass of brief mini-articles and ill-informed personal opinions. We can use the technological advantages to become a better-connected, more democratic society.

1. Underline the sentence that restates the thesis.

2. Circle the section that calls for the reader to take action.

3. Double underline the sentence that looks to the future.

Your Own Writing

Planning Your Conclusion

A. *What will you put in your conclusion? List your ideas here.*

_____

_____

B. *Write the sentence that will remind the reader of your thesis statement.*

_____

_____

C. *What strategy or strategies will you use to close the essay?*

_____

_____

D. Checking in. *Share your ideas with a partner. Did your partner . . .*

- choose an effective strategy?

- return to the idea in the thesis statement in a new and interesting way?

Writing Your First Draft

A. *Read the* Tip for Writers. *Review your notes on pages 36, 40, and 46–47. Then write the first draft of your essay. When you are finished, give your essay a working title.*

Tip for Writers

When you write your first draft, be sure that the purpose of your essay is clear.

B. *After you write the first draft, put in citations for any sources you used. Use MLA style to cite sources within and at the end of your essay.*

In-Text Citations: Cite any quotations, summaries, paraphrases, and other borrowed material at the end of the sentence in which the material appears. If you have given the author's name earlier in the sentence, you don't need to repeat it.

Examples:

Citing a Fact: In a 2009 issue of *The Nation,* a journalist and a media professor discussed a modest proposal to save journalism (Nichols and McChesney).

Citing a Paraphrase: One writer for *Sojourners* magazine claims that most independent investigative journalists in this country still work for daily newspapers (Collum).
   [or]
Danny Duncan Collum, a writer for *Sojourners* magazine, claims that most independent investigative journalists in this country still work for daily newspapers.

Citing a Quote: The legendary journalist said, "Here I am, 77, in this whole new medium of social networking and Twitter and all of that. And we used to do Twitter: We just sent them as Valentines when I was growing up" (Moyers).

A List of Works Cited: At the end of your writing, provide a list of all the sources you have cited. Type "Works Cited" at the top of the list and center the heading. Then organize your sources alphabetically according to the author's last name. If the source has no author, alphabetize it under the title. Indent the second line of the source.

The basic format for individual citations and a "Works Cited" list is shown below.

Examples:

Author. "Article Title." *Magazine Title* date: page no. medium. *(periodical)*

Author. *Book Title*. Publisher, date: page no. medium. *(book)*

Name of Interviewee. Personal Interview. date. *(personal interview)*

Name of Interviewee. Interview with Interviewer's Name. "Title of Interview." *website title*. Publisher, date. medium. date accessed. <URL>. *(online interview)*

website title. Publisher, date. medium. date accessed. <URL> *(website)*

Works Cited

Collum, Danny Duncan. "How to save journalism: can a government-subsidized press save democracy?" *Sojourners* June 2009: 40. Print.

Couturier, Jean. Personal Interview. 28 May 2011.

McChesney, Robert, and John Nichols. Interview with Amy Goodman and Juan Gonzalez. "The Death and Life of American Journalism." *democracynow.org*. Democracy Now, 4 Feb. 2010. Web. 18 July 2011.

Nichols, John, and Robert W. McChesney, "The Death and Life of Great American Newspapers." *The Nation* 6 Apr. 2009. Print.

For more information about research and citations, see the Appendix (pages 194–195). The format for citing other sources can also be found in MLA handbooks, on the websites of most college and university libraries in North America, or by searching the Internet using the keywords *MLA style*.

C. *Hand in your draft to your teacher.*

Revising your work is an essential part of the writing process. This is your opportunity to be sure that your essay has all the important pieces and that it is clear.

Focused Practice

A. *You have read parts of this persuasive essay already. Now read the entire essay and notice how the parts fit together.*

Advantages of the New Media

As the number of Internet users continues to grow, do you think that the Internet will change the way that we read and think about the news? As more and more people, especially young people, turn to the Internet for news about world and local events, we find that newspapers, television, and radio news have been losing their audience or even going out of business. Some people are concerned about this shift because newspapers provide important in-depth coverage of events, while some Internet news sites only report opinions or repeat what is already in the newspapers. However, the new media offer so many advantages over the traditional media that they could easily become better sources of news than any we have ever had.

We cannot deny that the traditional media have long served as excellent sources of news for societies around the world. Newspapers employ large staffs of reporters to investigate and report on politics, business, sports, entertainment, science, and the arts. Danny Duncan Collum, a writer for *Sojourners* magazine, claims that most independent investigative journalists in this country still work for daily newspapers. Newspapers are an important part of every community in a free society because readers trust them to challenge authority and report the truth. Television and radio news are popular and convenient ways to see and hear the latest news. The "seeing" on television is especially important. Videos of news events, such as violent crimes or wars, have a great deal of influence on public opinion. Many people feel that the traditional media simply cannot be replaced by the news available on computers and smart phones.

Why can't they? The new media are more convenient than the traditional media in several respects. Computers are in most American homes today, and laptops and netbooks are becoming more portable. Smart phones offer an application that provides the *New York Times* in any location. Even more available

(continued)

are the same videos of news events that are shown on television news, and many more. One of the most popular websites, YouTube, now has a significant effect on American culture. As we become able to record surrounding events at a moment's notice on our cell phone cameras, we can share them with the world. The average person now has more power to expose wrongdoing, such as police brutality. We can all become potential journalists.

In many other ways too, an important advantage of the new media is their interactivity. Most news stories are followed by comment sections on which readers can post their comments and respond to one another. Entries are often in the hundreds for major news. Sometimes the writer of the story responds to these comments with more information, turning the news report into an interactive community discussion. According to Claire Cain Miller of the *New York Times*, 25 percent of Internet news readers contribute to comment sections, and 80 percent email stories to their friends. Although some reader comments can be pointlessly argumentative and angry, most of them come from concerned citizens who wish to participate more fully in discussions of important news. The letters-to-the-editor section of traditional newspapers serves the same function but is not nearly as interactive. It is clear that better forums for citizen participation can only improve the quality of our government and our lives.

The new media are not only interactive, they are also interconnected. It is now possible for journalists, bloggers, and the rest of us to provide links to other stories on the Internet. These links are sprinkled through the news story itself or in a list at the end. With the ability of writers to support and contribute to one another's research, it is possible that Internet news sites won't need to take on as many reporters as daily papers have done in the past. If journalists from trusted websites are careful to provide links to other trusted sources, we will have better access to information and be introduced to new, interesting sources.

It is clear that the new media advantages in convenience, interactivity, and interconnectivity create a rich environment for the news. As the reading public, we need to make sure that we don't lose the advantages of the old media, especially the tradition of independent daily newspapers. We need to know where our news is coming from. We should demand the best investigative journalism from the

(continued)

sites we use. We can't let newspapers die off while the Internet becomes a mass of brief mini-articles and ill-informed personal opinions. We can use the technological advantages to become a better-connected, more democratic society.

Works Cited

Collum, Danny Duncan. "How to save journalism: can a government-subsidized press save democracy?" *Sojourners* June 2009: 40. Print.

Miller, Claire Cain. "The New News Junkie Is Online and On the Phone." *New York Times* 1 Mar. 2010. Print.

B. *Work with a partner. Answer the questions about "Advantages of the New Media."*

1. What is the thesis statement? Underline it.

2. Which paragraph gives the opposing point of view? Check (✓) it.

3. Which organization pattern does the essay follow?

   a. Organization 1: Begin the body by stating the opposing point of view.

   b. Organization 2: End the body by stating the opposing point of view.

   c. Organization 3: Add the opposing point of view to each paragraph when necessary.

4. Which advantage is discussed in paragraph 3? Underline the sentence that states it.

5. Which question provides a transition from paragraph 2 to paragraph 3? Circle it.

6. Which advantage is discussed in paragraph 4? Underline the sentence that states it.

7. Which phrase provides a transition from paragraph 3 to paragraph 4? Circle it.

8. Which advantage is discussed in paragraph 5? Underline the sentence that states it.

9. Which phrase provides a transition from paragraph 4 to paragraph 5? Circle it.

10. Find a paraphrase from another source. Circle the paraphrase and the citation.

11. Which sentence in the conclusion refers to the ideas in paragraphs 3, 4, and 5? Underline it.

C. Checking in. *Discuss your marked-up essays with another pair of students. Then in your group, share which argument you found most convincing in the essay. Explain your answer.*

Building Word Knowledge

The writer included many phrasal verbs in "Advantages of New Media," including *turn to, turn into, take on, make sure,* and *die off.*

Work with a partner. Use each phrasal verb in the list to replace a verb in one of the sentences. Be sure to use the correct tense and form of the verbs. The first one is done for you.

~~check out~~	hand out	keep up	take on	turn up

check out
1. Good reporters ~~investigate~~ every available source of information for a story.

2. New political websites are appearing all the time.

3. Some weekly newspapers are distributed for free on street corners.

4. Newspapers are likely to close if they can't continue their sales rates.

5. News websites may begin to hire more reporters as the websites grow.

Your Own Writing

Revising Your Draft

A. *Reread the first draft of your essay. Use the Revision Checklist to identify parts of your writing that might need improvement.*

B. *Review your plans and notes, and your responses to the Revision Checklist. Then revise your first draft. Save your revised essay. You will look at it again in the next section.*

Revision Checklist

Did you . . .

☐ make the purpose of your essay clear?

☐ use an opening strategy to get the reader's attention?

☐ express the controlling idea of the entire essay in your thesis statement?

☐ give enough background information in your introduction?

☐ include the opposing point of view (counterargument)?

☐ give enough facts, reasons, and examples to support your arguments?

☐ connect the parts of your essay with transitions?

☐ restate the thesis and use an effective concluding strategy?

☐ use any phrasal verbs in your essay?

☐ give your essay a good title?

☐ cite any sources that you used in your essay?

■ GRAMMAR PRESENTATION

Before you hand in your revised essay, you must check it for any errors in grammar, punctuation, and spelling. In this section, you will learn about indirect speech. You will focus on this grammar when you edit and proofread your essay.

Noun Clauses: Indirect Speech

Grammar Notes	Examples
1. We can **report speech** in two ways: direct speech and indirect speech. **Direct speech** (also called **quoted speech**) is the exact words of someone speaking. It is enclosed in quotation marks.	• Collum said, **"Lots of people are talking about this problem."**
Indirect speech (also called **reported speech**) is someone's report of direct speech. It does not contain the exact words of a speaker and is not enclosed in quotation marks. Indirect speech reports what a speaker said in a **noun clause** introduced by a reporting verb.	noun clause • Collum said **that lots of people were talking about that problem**.
If a statement is reported, the noun clause can be introduced by *that*. If a question is reported, the noun clause is introduced by *if*, *whether (or not)*, or a *wh-* question word.	noun clause • We need to know **where our news is coming from**.
2. Use a reporting verb such as **say**, **tell**, **claim** or **report**. When you use **say**, **claim**, or **report**, do not mention the listener or reader.	• Collum **said**, "The *Rocky Mountain News* in Denver has closed. Denver now has only one newspaper."
Remember that you often need to change the verb forms, pronouns, and some adverbs.	• My teacher says, "I **read** the paper every day."
When you use **tell**, mention the listener or reader.	• Collum **told us** that the *Rocky Mountain News* in Denver **had closed**. Denver **then had** only one newspaper.
When the reporting verb is in the simple present, present progressive, present perfect, or future, the verb in the noun clause does not change.	• My teacher says that **she reads** the paper every day.
We often do not change verbs to past forms if general truths are reported.	• She reported that the newspaper **is delivered** to our library every morning.

(continued)

3. To report **indirect *yes/no* questions**, use a noun clause beginning with *if* or *whether (or not)*. Use a reporting verb such as *ask* or *inquire*.

We often add an object (noun or pronoun) after the verb *ask*.

When you report a question that you ask yourself, use the verb *wonder*.

Use statement word order, not question word order, to report indirect *yes/no* questions.

- "Do you read international news on the Internet?"
- My classmate **asked** me **if I read international news on the Internet**.
  Nᴏᴛ: My classmate asked me ~~do I read international news on the Internet~~.

- "Will we have daily newspapers in twenty years?"
- I **wondered** whether **we would have daily newspapers in twenty years**.

4. To report ***wh-* questions**, use a noun clause beginning with a question word such as *why*, *where*, or *when*.

Use statement word order to report indirect questions about the predicate.

Use question word order to report indirect questions about the subject.

- "Where do the links on those sites lead you?"
- Collum asked **where the links on those sites led us**.

- "What is the best site for breaking news?"
- My classmate asked me **what the best site for breaking news is**.

- "Who is going to write about social media?"
- My teacher asked us **who was going to write about social media**.

Focused Practice

A. *Change each sentence from direct to indirect speech. You will need to add the name of a speaker or writer and the reporting verb. Instead of a name, you can use* the author, my classmate, *or another term.*

Statements

1. "The news about newspapers just keeps getting worse."

   The author said that the news about newspapers just keeps getting worse.

2. "The new media are more convenient than the traditional media."

   _____

   _____

3. "Chinese-language television is an excellent source of news about China." (Use *tell*.)

   _____

   _____

4. "We need to know where our news is coming from."

   _____

   _____

5. "Radio stations always have the local news right away."

_____

_____

Yes/No **Questions**

6. "Do most people subscribe to a daily newspaper?"

_____

_____

7. "Do you subscribe to a daily newspaper?"

_____

_____

8. "Is a newspaper available in your native language?"

_____

_____

9. "Have you seen my new video on YouTube?"

_____

_____

10. "Did the teacher assign an essay on social media?" (Use *wonder*.)

_____

_____

Wh- **Questions**

11. "Where do bloggers first see the stories?"

_____

_____

12. "Where is our news coming from?"

_____

_____

13. "Which national news television channel is the best?"

_____

_____

(continued)

14. "What are my classmates writing about?" (Use *wonder*.)

_____

_____

15. "What do we call a person who writes a web log?"

_____

_____

B. *Tell a partner about a recent conversation you had with a friend or classmate on a school-related topic, such as a class you are both taking. Use reported speech in your telling.*

C. *Read and edit the news story. There are seven mistakes in the use of noun clauses in direct and indirect speech. The first one is already corrected. Find and correct six more.*

Yesterday the government of Freedonia fell to a popular uprising in its capital city, Sopa de Pato. The president of Freedonia reports ~~us~~ that his administration has done everything to bring prosperity to the country, but the people of Freedonia seem to disagree. When we asked the president why does his family own all the successful businesses in the country, he merely pointed to towering photos of himself on all the exterior walls. "How can you expect the little people to compete with this magnificence?" he asked. The president wonders why do his people dislike his government, although he did say us that he didn't speak to any of his people for many years. The ruling political party has controlled the local media for 22 years, but today the television news is filled with protesters celebrating in the streets. One happy man asked us if that we could tell the world that a new day has reached Freedonia. He told that it was the best day of his life.

D. *Write five sentences related to the topic you chose on page 35. Use noun clauses. These may be sentences that are already in your essay.*

1. _____

_____

2. _____

_____

3. _____

_____

4. _____

_____

5. _____

_____

Your Own Writing

Editing Your Draft

A. *Use the Editing Checklist to edit and proofread your essay.*

B. *Prepare a clean copy of the final draft of your essay and hand it in to your teacher.*

Editing Checklist
Did you . . .
☐ include noun clauses and use them correctly?
☐ use correct verb forms, punctuation, and spelling?
☐ use phrasal verbs and other words correctly?

UNIT 3 Types of Intelligence

IN THIS UNIT You will be writing an essay about the similarities and differences in the types of intelligence shown by two people.

World leaders in politics and business have traditionally shared many common traits. For example, they have been ambitious and intelligent enough to rise to the top. But a close look will reveal very different kinds of people with different forms of intelligence. What kind of intelligence do you think is important for success?

Planning for Writing

▍BRAINSTORM

A. *Work with a partner to choose two political leaders or two business leaders that you both know. Choose one leader below and another one of your own.*

Political Leaders   **Business Leaders**

Mohandas Gandhi   Nelson Mandela   Oprah Winfrey   Donald Trump

B. Using a Venn Diagram. When you write about two topics, such as the two leaders you chose, you can use a graphic organizer like the Venn diagram at the bottom of the page to record similarities and differences between them.

Discuss with your partner which of the following words best describes each leader you chose.

articulate	caring	idealistic	scientific	thoughtful
artistic	friendly	intelligent	self-controlled	visionary
athletic	graceful	musical	sophisticated	warm

C. *Write your leaders' names in the Venn diagram. With your partner, use the diagram to list similarities and differences between Leaders 1 and 2. First, write words that apply to both of them. Then write words that only apply to each of them.*

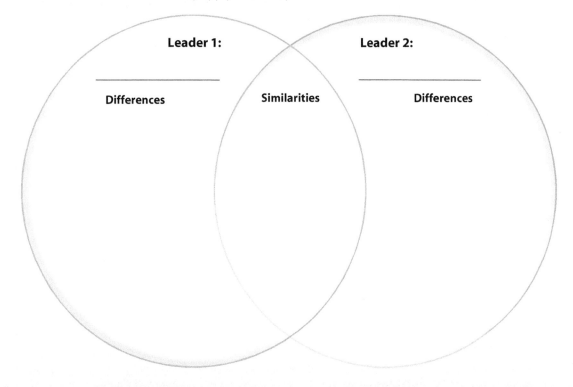

READ

Examine these items from an IQ test. Then read the excerpt from a psychology textbook.

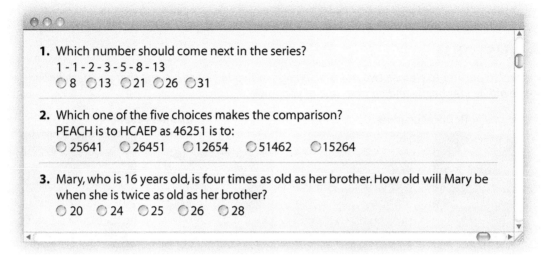

1. Which number should come next in the series?
   1 - 1 - 2 - 3 - 5 - 8 - 13
   ○ 8 ○ 13 ○ 21 ○ 26 ○ 31

2. Which one of the five choices makes the comparison?
   PEACH is to HCAEP as 46251 is to:
   ○ 25641 ○ 26451 ○ 12654 ○ 51462 ○ 15264

3. Mary, who is 16 years old, is four times as old as her brother. How old will Mary be when she is twice as old as her brother?
   ○ 20 ○ 24 ○ 25 ○ 26 ○ 28

Gardner's Multiple Intelligences

1   Look familiar? American children are often given IQ (Intelligence Quotient) tests in school in order to predict their academic ability. However, educators have always known that a single IQ score doesn't tell the whole story about a child's strengths and abilities. Psychologist Howard Gardner has rejected the view that there is a single entity called "intelligence." Rather, he believes there are different types of intelligence, called multiple intelligences, which vary from person to person. Gardner identifies eight different intelligences: *linguistic, logical-mathematical, musical, spatial, bodily-kinesthetic, interpersonal, intrapersonal,* and *naturalist.* These separate intelligences are believed to be independent of each other. Thus, a person could be high in some intelligences but low in others. For example, someone might have a high level of linguistic, or verbal, intelligence but a lower level of intelligence in mathematics, music, or spatial relationships. Some people have good "people skills" (interpersonal intelligence) but may not be highly skilled at mathematical and logical tasks.

2   Gardner's theory grew out of his work at the Boston Veteran's Administration Center,[1] where he closely observed patients with brain damage. He saw that because of brain damage, some people lose specific abilities but keep others. For instance, a patient who could no longer talk could still sing. Another patient who could no longer add and subtract could still interact with people socially. Gardner also examined child prodigies[2] who could perform extraordinarily well in music or math but were of normal ability in all other areas. In fact, children with certain forms of brain disorders can instantaneously[3] perform complex multiplication problems even though they cannot read or write. Gardner hypothesized[4] that these abilities must depend on different mental processes, and, therefore, are psychologically distinct[5] intelligences.

---

[1] **Veteran's Administration Center:** medical center for former soldiers, sailors, etc.
[2] **child prodigies:** children who are extraordinarily good at a particular activity
[3] **instantaneously:** happening immediately
[4] **hypothesize:** to make an educated guess
[5] **distinct:** separate

3   Gardner's theory of multiple intelligences has received criticism. Some critics point out that it does not explain how multiple intelligences interact with one another. Most cognitive[6] activities involve an interaction of multiple abilities, not just one type of intelligence. It is clear, as an example, that the ability to relate effectively to others (interpersonal intelligence) depends in part on the linguistic skills we need to express ourselves clearly (linguistic intelligence). Other critics wonder if the multiple intelligences are just another way of naming abilities or talents. Yet Gardner's theory has had enormous influence, especially in educational settings. Schools have enriched their programs in order to help children develop specific intelligences rather than focusing just on verbal and mathematical abilities. For example, teachers are now encouraged to design lessons that will appeal to spatial or kinesthetic learners.

4   Most of us have an "intelligence profile," with some strong areas on the following chart and some weak areas. How about you? Have you always found it easy to draw pictures but difficult to calculate the answers on math tests? Can you find your way around a forest? Do you always sing in tune? Use the following chart to determine your own intelligence profile.

Type of Intelligence	Description	Groups with High Levels of the Intelligence
Linguistic	Ability to understand and use words	Writers, poets, effective public speakers
Logical-mathematical	Ability to perform mathematical, computational, or logical operations	Scientists, engineers, computer programmers
Musical	Ability to analyze, compose, or perform music	Musicians, singers, composers
Spatial	Ability to perceive spatial relationships and arrange objects in space	Painters, architects, sculptors
Bodily-kinesthetic	Ability to control bodily movements and manipulate objects effectively	Dancers, athletes, race-car drivers, mechanics
Interpersonal	Ability to relate effectively to others and to understand others' moods and motives	Industrial and political leaders, effective supervisors
Intrapersonal	Ability to understand one's own feelings and behavior	Psychologically well-adjusted people
Naturalist	Ability to recognize objects and patterns in nature, such as flora and fauna	Botanists, biologists, naturalists

---

[6] **cognitive:** thinking

Source: From Nevid. PSYCHOLOGY, 1/e. Copyright © 2003 Wadsworth, a part of Cengage Learning, Inc. Reproduced by permission. www.cengage.com/permissions.

Building Word Knowledge

Using Word Families. To write well, it is important to learn all the members of a word family so that you can use the right form of the word. Here are some words from "Gardner's Multiple Intelligences," along with other members of their word families:

Examples:

Psychologist Howard Gardner has rejected the view that there is a single entity called **intelligence**.

intelligence (noun)   **intelligent** (adjective)   **intelligently** (adverb)

Rather, he believes there are different types of intelligence, called multiple intelligences, which **vary** from person to person.

vary (verb)   **various** (adjective)   **variously** (adverb)   **variety** (noun)

For example, the ability to **relate** effectively to others (interpersonal intelligence) depends in part on the linguistic skills needed to **express** oneself clearly (linguistic intelligence).

relate (verb)   **relation** (noun)   **relationship** (noun)

express (verb)   **expression** (noun)   **expressive** (adjective)

A. *Use your knowledge of grammar and vocabulary and your dictionaries to write other forms of the following words from the reading. There may be more than one correct answer for certain parts of speech.*

1. The model has received its share of **criticism**.

   criticism (noun)

   _____ adjective

   _____ adverb

   _____ verb

2. For example, a patient who could no longer talk could still sing, or a patient who could no longer add and subtract could still **interact** with people **socially**.

   interact (verb)   **socially** (adverb)

   _____ noun   _____ adjective

   _____ adjective   _____ verb

   _____ adverb   _____ noun

B. *The reading on pages 62–63 contains many words from common word families, including the ones listed below. Label each word* noun, adjective, *or* adverb. *Then circle the suffix (or word ending) that helps you know the part of speech. The first one is done for you.*

1. academic   *adjective*   4. effectively   _____

2. educators   _____   5. psychologically _____

3. musical   _____   6. naturalists   _____

Focused Practice

A. *Read the* Tip for Writers. *Then work with a partner to find explanations and examples in "Gardner's Multiple Intelligences." Make a list of the new ideas that needed explanations and examples.*

Tip for Writers

When writers introduce new ideas, they usually **provide an explanation or example** to help the reader understand them.

1. *multiple intelligences* _____

2. _____

3. _____

4. _____

5. _____

B. *Work with a partner. Add the following ideas, explanations, and examples to the correct sections of the chart below. The first one is done for you.*

1. ~~Some children who are good at math are not good at reading.~~

2. Some patients with brain damage can't talk, but they can still sing.

3. The multiple "intelligences" are nothing more than skills or talents.

4. Teachers try to create lessons that appeal to "kinesthetic learners."

5. Employees with good "people skills" often succeed in customer-service careers.

6. Many cognitive tasks demand more than one kind of intelligence.

7. Musical prodigies usually have normal abilities in other areas.

8. Schools enrich their programs with more music and art.

9. The IQ score doesn't tell the whole story about a child's ability to succeed.

Support for Gardner's Theory

Some children who are good at math are not good at reading.

Criticism of Gardner's Theory

Applications of Gardner's Theory

C. *Writers use a variety of transition words and expressions to introduce examples. Find two more phrases in the reading that are used to signal examples:*

Paragraph 1: _For example_

Paragraph 2: _____

Paragraph 3: _____

D. *Write about your own intelligence profile. Choose one or two types of intelligence from the reading, and write a paragraph explaining why you think you have this type (or these types) of intelligence.*

_____

_____

_____

_____

_____

_____

_____

_____

_____

_____

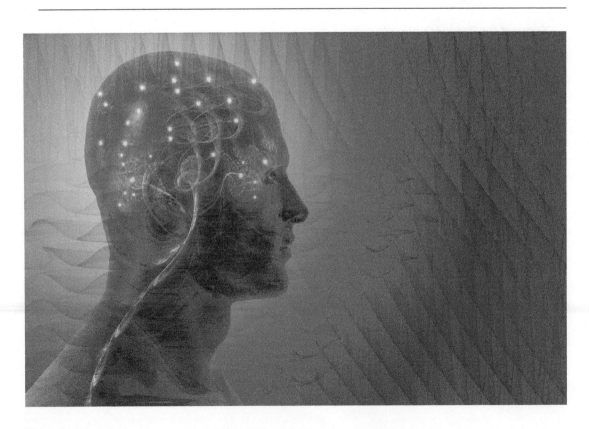

Writing a Compare-Contrast Essay

You are going to write an essay that compares and contrasts two people. Other subjects for a compare-contrast essay might include things or ideas like two schools, two careers, or two political systems. When you compare two people, you point out how they are alike. When you contrast two people, you point out how they are different. Your essay will do both.

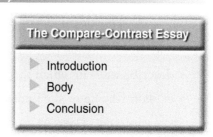

The Compare-Contrast Essay

▷ Introduction
▷ Body
▷ Conclusion

Like all essays, a compare-contrast essay has three parts.

Step 1 Prewriting

For a compare-contrast essay, the prewriting step involves selecting two people or things that have clear similarities and/or differences. It also includes brainstorming ideas to develop specific points of comparison and contrast. We'll use the phrase "points of comparison" to mean points of contrast as well.

Your Own Writing

Choosing Your Assignment

A. *Choose Assignment 1 or Assignment 2.*

1. Many different kinds of people become successful leaders in their fields. Choose two well-known people from the same field and compare and contrast their types of intelligence. Here are some categories you can choose from:

   • two award-winning actors

   • two popular musicians in the same musical genre (e.g., two rock or classical musicians)

   • two political leaders

   • two business leaders

2. Many different kinds of people become good teachers. Choose two of the best teachers you have ever had. Compare and contrast their types of intelligence and recommend one of them to another student.

B. *Freewrite for 10 minutes on your assignment. Here are some questions to get you started:*

   • What do you already know about the two people?

   • Why are these people interesting to you? What more do you want to find out about them?

C. Checking in. *Work with a partner who chose the same assignment. Discuss the ideas and details you wrote in Exercise B. Did your partner . . .*

- choose two people that have clear similarities and differences in their intelligences?

- describe ways in which their intelligences are alike and different?

- explain why he or she finds these people interesting?

Share your point of view on your partner's subjects. Based on your discussion, make changes and additions to your writing.

D. *Complete the Venn diagram. List the similarities and differences between the two people. Fill in as much information as you can. You will have a chance to review, change, or add information later in the unit.*

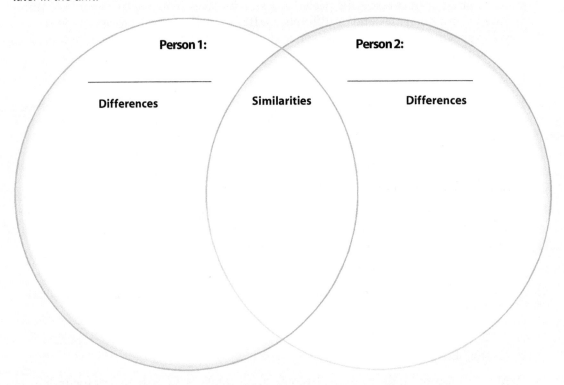

Person 1: _____

Differences

Similarities

Person 2: _____

Differences

Finding Out More

A. *Learn more about the two people you chose to compare and contrast in your essay.*

- If you chose Assignment 1, go online or to the library to research the two leaders you chose to write about. Make sure to check the biography section in the library.

  - For two artists, examine famous works—movies, paintings, or songs.

  - For two business leaders, examine successful products.

  - For two political leaders, examine memorable writings or speeches.

- If you chose Assignment 2, try to interview other students who were instructed by the teachers you chose to write about. Also, include your own memories as part of your research.

  - Draw a picture of the teacher.

  - Make a list of the teacher's qualities similar to the lists you prepared for a political or business leader on page 61.

  - Tell a story about a favorite lesson or day in class with your teacher.

  - Think about how you felt when you were a student in the teacher's class. How would you describe your feelings?

B. *Take notes on what you found out. For example:*

- Record key information about each person.

- Note the sources for your information.

- Record the names of the people you interviewed, the date of the interview, and any quotations you might want to use in your essay.

- Add relevant information to the Venn diagram on page 68.

Use this information when you write your essay.

C. Checking in. *Share your information with your partner. Did your partner . . .*

- gather enough facts and examples?

- use at least three reliable sources?

Step 2   Writing the First Draft

■ THE INTRODUCTION

In Unit 1, you learned that the introductory paragraph gives important background information to help the reader understand the thesis statement.

In a compare-contrast essay, the thesis statement usually identifies the two subjects being compared and contrasted and the points of comparison. It may also indicate the purpose of the comparison. It may be one sentence or two sentences.

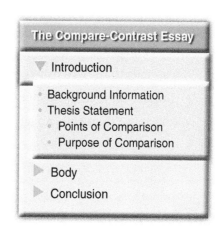

The Compare-Contrast Essay

▼ Introduction
- Background Information
- Thesis Statement
  - Points of Comparison
  - Purpose of Comparison

▶ Body
▶ Conclusion

In academic writing, you usually compare and contrast two subjects for a purpose:

- to demonstrate the superiority of one subject

- to make a recommendation or choice

- to point out underlying commonalities or distinctions

Before you begin writing, identify the purpose of your comparison and incorporate it in your thesis statement, if appropriate.

Types of Intelligence   **69**

To demonstrate the superiority of one subject:

Although Oprah Winfrey and Donald Trump have both demonstrated their interpersonal intelligence in successful businesses and television shows, Winfrey's heartfelt books, magazines, and interviews have made her more popular.

To make a recommendation or choice:

Both Ms. Smith and Ms. Lee are great biology teachers, but I would recommend Ms. Lee because of her ability on field trips to identify every plant and animal in the forest.

To point out underlying commonalities or distinctions:

Mohandas Gandhi and Nelson Mandela were both famous for their self-control and ability to inspire people. However, it is not so well known that they were both clever lawyers with highly developed analytical minds.

Focused Practice

A. *Read the following essay assignment. Then decide what kind of background information you might use for an introductory paragraph on the topic. Check (✓) the information you choose and discuss your choices with a partner.*

- Ask yourself this question to help you: *Is the information necessary?*

- Give reasons for your choices when you and your partner have different opinions.

Many different kinds of people become successful leaders in their fields. Choose two well-known business leaders and compare and contrast their types of intelligence.

_____ **1.** Information about the world of business

_____ **2.** Information about types of intelligence

_____ **3.** Information about the two business leaders you chose

_____ **4.** Information about the field of psychology

B. *Read the characteristics of a successful thesis statement.*

A successful thesis statement for a compare-contrast essay . . .

- presents the controlling idea of the entire essay and introduces the subjects that will be compared.

- responds to the assignment.

- contains an idea the writer will develop and support.

- does more than state a fact; usually presents an arguable assertion or claim.

Now check (✓) the sentences that would make a good thesis statement for the essay assignment in Exercise A. Explain your choices to a partner.

_____ **1.** I chose two of the most famous business leaders in history for my essay.

_____ **2.** Although Bill Gates and Steve Jobs are both mathematical geniuses, Gates has shown more intrapersonal intelligence through his devotion to charity.

_____ **3.** As founders of successful technology companies, Eric Schmidt of Google and Mark Zuckerberg of Facebook both demonstrate logical-mathematical intelligence. However, Zuckerberg's lack of interpersonal skills seems to have caused him many problems.

_____ **4.** Bill Gates and Steve Jobs are both extremely intelligent.

_____ **5.** Steve Jobs has logical-mathematic, interpersonal, and spatial intelligence.

C. *Read the model introductory paragraph for an essay on the assignment in Exercise A. Discuss the questions with a partner.*

> Bill Gates, the founder of Microsoft, and Steve Jobs, the founder of Apple Computer, are both well-known pioneers in technology who have changed the world through their inventions. Both men have also built large companies to produce and market those inventions, and both have been criticized for their management styles. But it's difficult to argue with this degree of success. Microsoft products are used in computers all over the world. Whenever Apple comes out with a new product, people line up for hours outside every Apple store. How did these two college dropouts become so influential? Gates and Jobs have both succeeded largely because of their logical-mathematical and interpersonal intelligences. However, Steve Jobs has been able to reach the public in a different way with his highly developed sense of spatial design.

1. Why do you think the writer chose these two business leaders?

2. Which kind of background information from Exercise A did the writer include?

3. Why do you think the writer included this kind of information?

4. Could the writer have included other kinds of information as background? If so, which other kinds?

5. Underline the thesis statement (one or two sentences).

Your Own Writing

Planning Your Introduction

A. *List the background information you will need to include in your introduction.*

_____

_____

_____

B. *Write a draft of your thesis statement. Make sure your thesis statement introduces the two people and the points of comparison your essay will discuss. It might also state the purpose of your comparison. Look back at your freewriting and Venn diagram to help you.*

_____

_____

C. Checking in. *Share your thesis statement with a partner. Does your partner's thesis statement . . .*

- present the controlling idea of the entire essay?

- respond to the assignment?

- contain a comparison he or she will develop in the essay?

- state more than a fact? Does it present an arguable assertion or claim?

- give you an idea about the purpose of the comparison?

Tell your partner what kind of supporting evidence you expect to see in his or her essay, based on the thesis statement. Based on your partner's feedback, you may want to rewrite your thesis statement.

■THE BODY

A comparison-contrast essay can be organized by the *block method* or the *point-by-point method*. In the block method, you discuss Subject A and then Subject B. In the point-by-point method, you compare and contrast Subject A and Subject B on a series of points. You may choose either method for your compare-contrast essay. There are two ways you could organize the body paragraphs for the introductory paragraph on page 71. Notice that you do not have to cover all three points of comparison for both subjects.

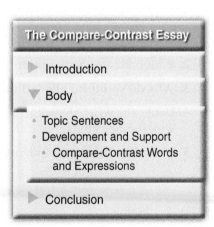

The Compare-Contrast Essay

▶ Introduction

▼ Body

- Topic Sentences
- Development and Support
  - Compare-Contrast Words and Expressions

▶ Conclusion

Example:

Essay Assignment: Many different kinds of people become successful leaders in their fields. Choose two well-known business leaders and compare and contrast their types of intelligence.

Block Method	Point-by-Point Method

Block Method

Body Paragraph 1: Bill Gates

    A. Logical-mathematical intelligence

    B. Interpersonal intelligence

Body Paragraph 2: Steve Jobs

    A. Logical-mathematical intelligence

    B. Interpersonal intelligence

    C. Spatial intelligence

Point-by-Point Method

Body Paragraph 1: Logical-mathematical intelligence

    A. Bill Gates

    B. Steve Jobs

Body Paragraph 2: Interpersonal intelligence

    A. Bill Gates

    B. Steve Jobs

Body Paragraph 3: Spatial intelligence

    Steve Jobs

Developing Body Paragraphs

In a compare-contrast essay, it is important to develop your assertions with as many specific descriptions and examples as possible. You not only need to *state*, or *tell*, the reader what you mean, but you also need to add sentences to *show* the reader. Here are some examples.

Telling Statements	Showing Statements
My daughter has a highly developed musical intelligence.	My daughter can learn a new Chopin piano sonata in a few days and play it from memory within a week. When she sings, she hits every note perfectly.
Steve Jobs is famous for creating innovative products.	When Steve Jobs creates a new product, such as the iPhone or iPad, fans all over the world grow so excited that they line up for hours at Apple stores, hoping for a chance to be one of the first buyers.

Focused Practice

A. *Underline the specific information and examples in the following paragraph from "Gardner's Multiple Intelligences." The first one is done for you.*

> Gardner's theory grew out of his work at the Boston Veteran's Administration Center, where he closely observed patients with brain damage. He saw that because of brain damage, some people lose specific abilities but keep others. For instance, a patient who could no longer talk could still sing, or a patient who could no longer add and subtract could still interact with people socially. Gardner also examined child prodigies, who could perform extraordinarily well in music or math
>
> *(continued)*

but were of normal ability in all other areas. In fact, children with certain forms of brain disorders can instantaneously perform complex multiplication problems even though they cannot read or write. Gardner hypothesized that these abilities must depend on different mental processes, and, therefore, are psychologically distinct intelligences.

B. *Complete the* **telling** *statements with your own information. Then write* **showing** *sentences to provide specific information and examples to support them.*

1. Tell: I am proud of my _____ intelligence.

Show: _____

2. Tell: My friend _____ is known for his/her ability to _____.

Show: _____

3. Tell: My friend _____ has excellent people skills.

Show: _____

4. Tell: Unlike me, my father/mother/sister/brother is a good _____.

Show: _____

5. Tell: In the future, I want to develop my ability to _____.

Show: _____

Using Compare-Contrast Words and Expressions

Many words and expressions can be used to signal similarities and differences. You may use them in your topic sentences or within paragraphs.

Examples:

Prepositions are followed by noun phrases:

prep.   noun phrase
Despite his lack of kinesthetic intelligence, Mr. Johnson possessed the people skills to be an effective basketball coach in my high school.

prep.   noun phrase
Like many other teachers, Ms. Smith enjoyed spending her time with young people.

Introductory adverbs are followed by independent clauses:

As military generals, Ulysses S. Grant and Dwight D. Eisenhower both used logical-mathematical

adverb   independent clause
intelligence. However, Grant's lack of interpersonal skills made him a poor president.

adverb   independent clause
Bill Gates dropped out of Harvard to start his own business. Similarly, Steve Jobs saw no reason to stay in school when he could be more creative in the business world.

Subordinate conjunctions begin dependent clauses:

sub. conj.   dependent clause
Although Steve Jobs is famous for his bad temper, his employees still rate him one of the best bosses.

sub. conj.   dependent clause
Just as music teachers love to listen to good music, English teachers love to read good books.

The word ***both*** can show similarities as an adjective, a pronoun, and a correlative conjunction, paired with *and*.

adjective
Both music teachers in my high school played the trumpet.

pronoun
Both loved to sing.

correlative conjunction
Both English teachers **and** history teachers love to read.

Focused Practice

Study the chart below. Then write sentences showing the similarities or differences between people you know. Use a preposition, an introductory adverb, a subordinate conjunction, or the word **both**. *Share your sentences with a partner or the class. The first sentence is done for you.*

Prepositions	Introductory Adverbs	Subordinate Conjunctions
compared to	also	although
despite/in spite of	conversely	despite the fact that
in addition to	however	even though
instead of	in the same way	just as
like	on the contrary	whereas
unlike	on the other hand	while
	similarly	

1. Two family members:

   Unlike my sister, who never studies, I stay up late every night laboring over

   English essays and chemistry lab reports.

2. Two friends:

   _____

   _____

3. Two family members:

   _____

   _____

(continued)

4. Two neighbors:

_____

_____

5. Two classmates:

_____

_____

6. Two movie stars:

_____

_____

Your Own Writing

Planning Your Body Paragraphs

A. _Before you begin writing your body paragraphs, complete one of the outlines below._

- Copy your thesis statement from page 72.

- Review the two ways to organize a compare-contrast essay on page 73.

- Select the method and number of paragraphs best suited to your topic. If you want to experiment with more than one method of organization, complete both outlines.

Compare-Contrast Essay

▶ Thesis Statement: _____

_____

Block Method

▶ Body Paragraph 1: Subject A

   ▶ Topic Sentence: _____

     _____

     ▶ Supporting Details:

       • _____

       • _____

       • _____

▶ Body Paragraph 2: Subject B

    ▶ Topic Sentence: _____

    _____

        ▶ Supporting Details:

            • _____

            • _____

            • _____

Point-by-Point Method

▶ Body Paragraph 1: Point 1

    ▶ Topic Sentence: _____

    _____

        ▶ Supporting Details:

            • _____

            • _____

            • _____

▶ Body Paragraph 2: Point 2

    ▶ Topic Sentence: _____

    _____

        ▶ Supporting Details:

            • _____

            • _____

            • _____

▶ Body Paragraph 3: Point 3 (Optional)

    ▶ Supporting Details:

            • _____

            • _____

            • _____

B. Checking in. *Share your outline with a partner. Did your partner...*

- choose the method that will work best for his or her essay, block or point-by-point?

- choose an appropriate subject (A or B) to discuss first, if he or she is using the block method?

- order the points of comparison appropriately, if he or she is using the point-by-point method?

- provide interesting supporting details?

Based on your partner's feedback, you may want to rewrite parts of your outline.

■ THE CONCLUSION

The concluding paragraph wraps up your essay. In a compare-contrast essay, your conclusion should leave your readers with a clear sense of your comparison and its significance.

To conclude your essay, return to the ideas in the thesis statement without repeating the same words. In the essay comparing the kinds of intelligence of two business leaders, you would include the names of the two business leaders and their forms of intelligence. Then before writing the rest of the conclusion, ask yourself some of these questions:

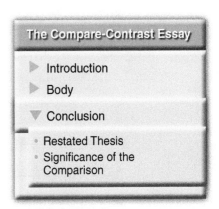

The Compare-Contrast Essay

▷ Introduction
▷ Body
▽ Conclusion
  • Restated Thesis
  • Significance of the Comparison

1. Why is the comparison important? Why are people interested in these two subjects?

2. Why am I making this comparison? To demonstrate the superiority of one subject over the other? To make a recommendation to someone? To explain my own preference for one or the other?

Your conclusions should leave your reader with a strong sense of the purpose of your essay.

Focused Practice

Read the following essay assignment and thesis statement. Then complete the following exercise.

Essay Assignment: Many different kinds of people become successful leaders in their fields. Choose two well-known business leaders and compare and contrast their types of intelligence.

Thesis Statement: Gates and Jobs have both succeeded largely because of their logical-mathematical and interpersonal intelligences. However, Jobs has been able to reach the public in a different way with his highly developed sense of spatial design.

Check (✓) all the items that give important reasons for comparing and contrasting the two subjects. Explain to your partner why these ideas should be in the conclusion.

_____ **1.** The differences among business leaders can explain the differences in products.

_____ **2.** I personally love Apple products.

_____ **3.** Business leaders in the same field can still be different in important ways.

_____ **4.** Certain types and combinations of intelligence can lead to great success.

_____ **5.** The inventions of both men will continue to influence our lives in the future.

_____ **6.** Bill Gates is a great philanthropist.

Your Own Writing

Planning Your Conclusion

A. *What will you put in your conclusion? List your ideas here.*

_____

_____

B. *Write the sentence that will remind the reader of your thesis statement.*

_____

_____

C. *What strategy or strategies will you use to close the essay?*

_____

_____

D. Checking in. *Share your ideas with a partner. Did your partner . . .*

- choose an effective strategy?

- discover a new and interesting way to phrase his or her thesis statement?

- make the significance of the comparison clear?

Writing Your First Draft

A. *Read the* Tip for Writers. *Review your notes on pages 68, 72, and 76–77. Then write the first draft of your essay. When you are finished, give your essay a working title.*

> **Tip for Writers**
>
> When you write your first draft, be sure that you provide explanations and examples to make your ideas clear.

B. *After you write the first draft, put in citations for any sources you used. Use MLA style for the in-text citations and "Works Cited" list. See Unit 2 pages 49–50 and the Appendix on pages 194–195 for more information on MLA style.*

C. *Hand in your draft to your teacher.*

Revising your work is an important part of the writing process. This is your opportunity to be sure that your essay has all the important pieces and that it is clear.

Focused Practice

A. *You have read parts of this compare-contrast essay already. Now read the entire essay to see how the parts fit together.*

The Brains Behind Computers

Bill Gates, the founder of Microsoft, and Steve Jobs, the founder of Apple Computer, are both well-known pioneers in technology who have changed the world through their inventions. Both men have also built large companies to produce and market those inventions, and both have been criticized for their management styles. But it's difficult to argue with this degree of success. Computers all over the world use Microsoft products. Whenever Apple comes out with a new product, people line up for hours outside every Apple store. How did these two college dropouts become so influential? Gates and Jobs have both succeeded largely because of their logical-mathematical and interpersonal intelligences. However, Steve Jobs has been able to reach the public in a different way with his highly developed sense of spatial design.

One of the reasons for the success of Microsoft is the ability of its founder, Bill Gates, to outsmart the competition. His intelligence profile, using the Gardner model of multiple intelligences, shows both mathematical-logical and interpersonal intelligence in his business dealings. Gates's mathematical-logical intelligence became apparent at an early age when he was excused from his eighth-grade math class to program the school's computer. Although Gates didn't complete his degree at Harvard, he was able to serve as the chief software architect at Microsoft. For the first five years, Gates reviewed every line of software code at Microsoft and personally wrote a great deal of it. Gates was also able to use his interpersonal intelligence to build his company. Despite being criticized for his aggressive management style, Gates has gotten results from his team and has defended his company against the competition and a long lawsuit from the U.S. government (Stross).

Like Bill Gates, Steve Jobs is famous for his mathematical-logical and interpersonal intelligence in creating and promoting his company's products.

And like Gates, Jobs also skipped out on a college degree in favor of using his mathematical-logical skills to start a technology company. Jobs also has remarkable interpersonal intelligence in handling people and making business deals that keep Apple ahead of its competition. Even though Jobs is known as a demanding boss who expects hard work and complete loyalty, he was given a 97 percent approval rating by his employees. He was the highest rated CEO in the United States in a 2010 survey by glassdoor.com. However, unlike Gates, Jobs has used his artistic genius to make the products special. Apple products, such as the Mac computers, the iPhone, and the iPod, are known for revolutionizing the market with their new technologies and attractive designs. For example, after the first Macintosh computers came out, other computer makers began to design attractive computers rather than ugly boxes. In his biography *iCon*, Jobs said, "I think what I'm best at is creating new, innovative products" (Simon and Young 120). Jobs, who hasn't limited his work to Apple Computers, is also one of the founders of Pixar Studios, the makers of such popular films as *Toy Story* and *Finding Nemo*. At Pixar, Jobs has used his spatial intelligence in the field of computer animation.

The intellectual strengths of these two business leaders, Bill Gates and Steve Jobs, can be seen in their products, their companies, and in the technology that we use every day. While both have led innovations in technology, Steve Jobs has also had a great influence on the artistic design of technological products. It will be interesting to see how the technological products and designs of the future will build on the work of these two men.

Works Cited

"Glassdoor Reveals Top 50 Best Places to Work, 2010: Southwest Airlines Ranked #1." *glassdoor.com.* glassdoor.com, 15 Dec. 2009. Web. 22 Aug. 2011.

Stross, Randall E. *The Microsoft Way: The Real Story of How the Company Outsmarts Its Competition.* New York: Basic Books, 1996. Print.

Young, Jeffrey S. and William L. Simon. *iCon Steve Jobs: The Greatest Second Act in the History of Business.* Hoboken: Wiley & Sons, 2006. Print.

B. *Work with a partner. Answer the questions about the essay.*

1. What is the thesis statement (one or two sentences)? Underline it.

2. How is this essay organized? _____

3. Who is the topic of paragraph 2? Double underline his name.

(continued)

4. Who is the topic of paragraph 3? Double underline his name.

5. Find specific details about each of these people that show us what they are like. Check (✓) them.

6. What compare-contrast word begins a body paragraph and connects the two paragraphs? Underline it.

7. Find other compare-contrast words in the essay and circle them.

8. What strategy is used in the conclusion? _____ Underline the sentence that uses this strategy.

C. Checking in. *Discuss your marked-up essays with another pair of students. Then in your group, share what you found most interesting about the essay. Explain your answer.*

Building Word Knowledge

The essay "The Brains Behind Computers" contains many words with large word families.

A. *Complete each sentence with the correct form of the word. Use a dictionary if necessary.*

1. Many competitors in the software industry have been _____ of Microsoft.

   a. criticize

   b. critical

   c. critically

   d. critic

2. Young people who want to _____ in the technology business should study the careers of Bill Gates and Steve Jobs.

   a. success

   b. successful

   c. succeed

   d. successfully

3. Gates and Jobs are both _____ business leaders.

   a. intelligent

   b. intelligence

   c. intelligences

   d. intelligently

4. Apple products _____ a lot of attention with their innovative technology and artistic design.

   a. attraction

   b. attractive

   c. attract

   d. attractively

B. *Here are more words from "The Brains Behind Computers." First, write a different form of the word and its part of speech in parentheses. Then write a sentence using the new word.*

Example:

produce (verb)

Both men also built large companies to produce and market those inventions.

product (noun)

Some Apple products are expensive.

1. artistic (adjective)

Jobs has used his **artistic** genius to make the products special.

_____

_____

2. complete (verb)

Gates didn't **complete** his degree at Harvard.

_____

_____

3. technology (noun)

Both men have led innovations in **technology**.

_____

_____

Your Own Writing

Revising Your Draft

A. *Reread the first draft of your essay. Use the Revision Checklist to identify parts of your writing that might need improvement.*

B. *Review your plans and notes, and your responses to the Revision Checklist. Then revise your first draft. Save your revised essay. You will look at it again in the next section.*

Revision Checklist

Did you . . .

☐ express the controlling idea of the essay in your thesis statement?

☐ give enough background information in your introduction?

☐ organize the essay with either the block or point-by-point method?

☐ make your ideas clear with enough explanations and examples?

☐ give enough details to develop and support your controlling ideas?

☐ connect the ideas in your essay with compare-contrast words and expressions?

☐ restate the controlling idea of the essay in your conclusion?

☐ use an effective concluding strategy?

☐ use the correct forms of words in your essay?

☐ give your essay a good title?

☐ cite any sources you used in your essay?

■ GRAMMAR PRESENTATION

Before you hand in your revised essay, you must check it for any errors in grammar, punctuation, and spelling. In this section, you will learn about adjective clauses. You will focus on this grammar when you edit and proofread your essay.

Adjective Clauses

Grammar Notes	Examples
1. A sentence with an adjective clause can be seen as a combination of two sentences.	*Howard Gardner is a psychologist + He developed the theory of multiple intelligences =* • Howard Gardner is a psychologist **who developed the theory of multiple intelligences**.
2. An adjective clause is a **dependent clause**. It modifies a noun or a pronoun in a main clause.	• There are different types of intelligence, **which vary from person to person**.
An adjective clause often begins with a **relative pronoun**: *who*, *whom*, *which*, or *that*. It can also begin with *whose*, *when*, or *where*. The word that begins an adjective clause usually comes directly after the noun or pronoun the clause modifies.	
An adjective clause can occur after a main clause or inside a main clause.	• Gardner worked at the Boston Veteran's Administration Center, **where he closely observed patients with brain damage**. • A patient **who could no longer talk** could still sing.
3. To refer to people, use *who* or *that* as the subject of verbs in adjective clauses.	• Naturalists are **people that** are able to recognize objects and patterns in nature. • A linguist is a **scholar who** studies language.
To refer to things, use *which* or *that* as the subject of verbs in adjective clauses.	• **IQ tests, which** are supposed to identify academic potential, are often given in schools. • Intelligence is a **topic that** has interested many psychologists.
The verb in an adjective clause agrees with the noun or pronoun the clause modifies.	• The **loss** of ability **that results** from brain damage is sometimes temporary. • **Tests** that **measure** intelligence are called IQ tests.

(continued)

4. To refer to people, use *whom* or *that* as the **object** of verbs in adjective clauses.

- **Dancers and athletes, whom** we admire for their grace, demonstrate bodily-kinesthetic intelligence.
- The **teachers that** I admire most are good public speakers.

To refer to things, use *which* or *that* as the **object** of verbs in adjective clauses.

- The **IQ test which** the students took last week contained 50 questions.
- The **IQ test that** the students took last week was difficult.

In conversation and informal writing, you can sometimes omit the relative pronoun if it is an object.

- The **IQ test** the students took last week is common in U.S. schools.

5. Use *whose* to introduce an adjective clause that indicates **possession**. We use *whose* to replace *his / her / its / their* + noun. An adjective clause with *whose* can modify people or things.

People often become writers or public speakers + Their linguistic intelligence is strong =
- People **whose linguistic intelligence** is strong often become writers or public speakers.

It is a psychological test + Its origins go back many years =
- It is a psychological test **whose origins** go back many years.

6. You can use *where* to introduce an adjective clause that modifies a noun of **place**. *Where* replaces the word *there*.

*The Boston Veteran's Administration Center is the place + Gardner developed his theory **there** =*
- The Boston Veteran's Administration Center is the place **where Gardner developed his theory**.

You can use *when* or *that* to begin an adjective clause that modifies a noun of time. You can omit *when* and *that* in this type of adjective clause.

- I can't think of a time **when/that I wasn't studying for tests**.
- I can't think of a time **I wasn't studying for tests**.

7. An adjective clause that distinguishes one person or thing from another is called **identifying** or essential. The clause is not enclosed in commas.

- The IQ test **that/which I took as a child** was the Stanford-Binet.

An adjective clause that adds extra information but does not distinguish one person or thing from another is called **nonidentifying** or nonessential. The clause is enclosed in commas.

- The Stanford-Binet IQ test**, which I took as a child,** has been criticized for cultural bias.

Focused Practice

A. *Look at the notes the school psychologist took on the fifth-grade students at Apple Valley School. Then write sentences about the children and their types of intelligence. Use adjective clauses. The first sentence is done for you.*

Apple Valley Fifth Grade Students

1.	Juan Ramirez	Leads the class in singing, plays guitar
2.	Craig Stephen	Programs the school computers
3.	Emma Boss	Is always happy and cheerful
4.	Anh Nguyen	Writes stories and recites poems for the class
5.	Veronica Saenz	Painted a mural on the wall of the school playground
6.	Benny Li	Plays soccer and basketball

1. *Juan Ramirez, who leads the class in singing and plays guitar, demonstrates musical intelligence.*

2. _____

_____

3. _____

_____

4. _____

_____

5. _____

_____

6. _____

_____

B. *Complete the teacher's report by forming adjective clauses. Add commas where necessary. The first sentence is done for you.*

My fifth grade class is having a great year. I have several students

_____who love to play sports_____. We're lucky to have a new playground
     1. (they love to play sports)

_____. Veronica, _____
    2. (we can play soccer and basketball there)   **3. (we gave her the task of painting a mural)**

drew pictures of sports teams and scientists. The school is grateful to the parents

_____. The student _____
    4. (their donations made it possible)   **5. (he programs the school computer)**

created interesting games for the children to practice math skills when the weather isn't

nice enough to go outside. The children also enjoy working in the school garden,

_____.
    6. (it provides fresh vegetables for snacks)

C. *Read and edit the paragraph. There are seven mistakes in the use of adjective clauses. The first one is already corrected. Find and correct six more.*

    The theory of multiple intelligences may not be universally accepted in the
                                                      who
field of psychology, but it is very popular among educators, ~~whom~~ have long
noticed that IQ tests don't predict excellence in every subject. Children love to read
can't always do difficult math problems, and the children with logical-mathematical
intelligence may not be gifted in tasks who require eye-hand coordination.
Teachers need to encourage children to develop their special forms of intelligence,
but they also might need to provide extra help for children which show no interest
in important subjects. It is also important for schools to provide opportunities for
students who's intelligence is musical or spatial to have an opportunity to discover
their talent. In the United States, where has many students from different cultures,
teachers try to guide each student to learn in the best way, that is probably not the
same way for all.

D. *Write five sentences related to the assignment you chose on page 67. Use adjective clauses. These may be sentences you already have in your essay.*

1. _____

_____

2. _____

_____

3. _____

_____

4. _____

_____

5. _____

_____

Your Own Writing

Editing Your Draft

A. *Use the Editing Checklist to edit and proofread your essay.*

B. *Prepare a clean copy of the final draft of your essay and hand it in to your teacher.*

Editing Checklist
Did you . . .
☐ include adjective clauses and form them correctly?
☐ use correct verb forms, punctuation, and spelling?
☐ use the correct forms of words (adjectives, adverbs, verbs, nouns)?

UNIT 4 Crime

IN THIS UNIT You will be writing an essay about the causes and effects of crime.

The Internet has made shopping, banking, and other financial transactions easy and convenient for consumers. At the same time, it has created opportunities for criminals to steal private information, money, and even the identities of millions of victims around the world. What do you think it would be like if someone stole your identity?

Planning for Writing

■ BRAINSTORM

A. Using a Brainstorming Map. *Why do you think the crime of identity theft is growing? What might be the causes of the crime? Work with a partner to create a brainstorming map of possible* **causes.**

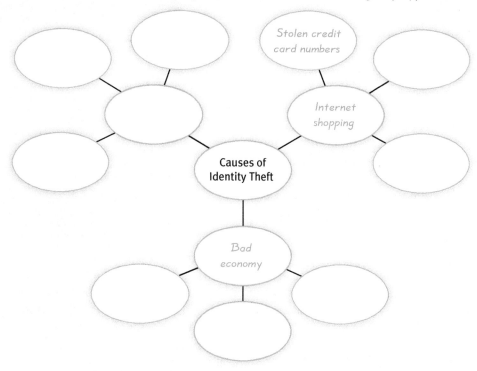

B. *In what ways can identity theft harm the victim and society? Work with a partner to create a brainstorming map of possible* **effects.**

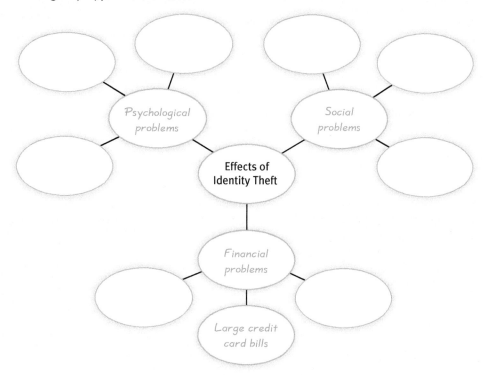

Identity fraud nightmare: One man's story

Technology and the recession push ID theft and fraud to record levels

By Jennifer Waters, MarketWatch

1 CHICAGO (MarketWatch.com)—Identity theft and fraud have ruined Dave Crouse's life.

2 In fewer than six months, some $900,000 in merchandise, gambling and telephone-services were charged to his debit card. His attempts to save his finances have cost him nearly $100,000 and have used up all his savings and retirement accounts. His credit score, once a strong 780, is now barely 500. And his identity—Social Security number, address, phone numbers, even historical information—is still being used in attempts to open credit cards and bank accounts.

3 "I have no identity," said Crouse, 56. "My identity is public knowledge and even though it's ruined, they're still using it," he said. "It ruined me financially and emotionally."

4 Crouse is among the 11.1 million adults—one in every 20 U.S. adults—last year who broke the record of the number of identity-fraud victims in the U.S., according to a recent study by Javelin Strategy and Research. That figure is up 12% over 2008 and is 37% ahead of 2007. The cost to all the victims: $54 billion. "The odds have never been higher for becoming a fraud victim," said James Van Dyke, Javelin president. "It's an easy crime to perpetrate,[1] a crime that's almost impossible to catch when done in a sophisticated manner and a crime in which law enforcement is very limited."

Endless paperwork

5 Crouse can prove the truth of that. Once an enthusiastic fan of online shopping and banking, the Bowie, Md., resident would sell things on eBay.com, an online auction site, download songs from iMesh.com and use his ATM card like a credit card. He first noticed unusual activity in his account in February of 2009 for small charges of $37 or $17.98. "All of a sudden it really got bad," he said. "In August the charges hit big time[2]—$600, $500, $100, $200—all adding up from $2,800 to $3,200 in one day."

6 He called his bank immediately and started what began a tiresome process of filling out what he said finally amounted to about 20 legal documents swearing that he was not responsible for the charges. He said one day he filled out a legal document about a charge and the next day the bank had accepted similar charges approaching $4,000. "At that point I was going to the bank every day and looking at everything," he said.

7 He opened a new account at a new bank, and the next day both accounts received a $1,100 charge. The new bank told him it was keystroke malware that had likely done him in.[3] Someone had hacked into[4] one of the sites he visited regularly; his computer got infected and picked up all his personal information by tracking every key he struck.

---

[1] **perpetrate:** to do something wrong or criminal
[2] **big time:** in a significant or serious way
[3] **done him in:** caused him great harm
[4] **hacked into:** illegally entered a computer system

8   While much of the fraud came from online purchases and at gambling sites, there were new accounts opened in different names but linked to his bank account. There was one purchase of a plasma TV from a Best Buy in Florida that was shipped to a Brooklyn, N.Y. address. In another case a woman in North Carolina was writing out checks tied to his account.

High-value targets

9   Identity thieves steal mostly through two means, according to Michael Stanfield, chief executive of Intersections Inc., a risk-management firm. They take an established address and phone number of an identity that "has some value," he said, like a doctor or a lawyer. In many instances, they can go to the Internet and acquire the matching Social Security number for as little as $50. They then have enough information to get an address changed with your bank account or a credit card account. They apply for new accounts as you.

10 Others take over existing accounts, Stanfield said, through keystroke malware that you have picked up through the Internet. Listening software then sits on your computer, waking up when you go to a bank site. It copies all your key strokes—your user name, password, challenge question, account numbers, everything.

11 "You leave and the bad guy goes right back in behind you," Stanfield said. "We've seen examples where that has occurred and it gets fixed and a month later the computer gets attacked again and he becomes a new victim, even with a new account. It's a horrible event, happening every minute of the day to someone," Stanfield said.

No one is completely protected

12 Identity theft affects people of all age and income levels. But those most at risk are those who spend the most and that tends to be middle-income families. Those most likely to miss fraud are usually 18 to 24 years old, simply because they don't pay enough attention to their accounts and, although most are technologically savvy, they're not protecting themselves against the worst of technology through malware and viruses. "The more you transact, the more you're at risk because you leave a trail behind," Van Dyke said.

13 As for Crouse, the trouble extended into other areas of his life. He was late paying bills and was charged with late fees, higher interest costs and penalties. One of his sons dropped out of college and another is reconsidering where he'll go because of costs. Crouse's advice: Don't touch websites that offer free things or 30-day trials; never give out personal information; and always keep your receipts.

Building Word Knowledge

Using Collocations. To write well, choose words and expressions that convey your meaning accurately and naturally. Here are some examples of collocations from "Identity fraud nightmare: One man's story."

public knowledge: information that is available to anyone

savings account: a bank account that is used to save money and earn interest

credit score: a numerical rating of someone's financial reliability used by banks and lenders

law enforcement: the actions taken by police to make sure laws are obeyed

personal information: private data such as someone's age, address, phone number, and email address

Find the collocations in the article on page 92. Notice how they are used.

Focused Practice

A. *Read the* **Tip for Writers.** *Work with a partner. Discuss the events in* "Identity fraud nightmare: One man's story." *Then, on your own, write one or two sentences summarizing the man's story.*

_____

_____

> **Tip for Writers**
>
> When you write about causes and effects, you need to **make time and cause-effect relationships clear**.

B. *When you write about causes and effects, it is important to make the sequence of events clear. Number the events in Dave Crouse's story in the order in which they occurred. The first event is numbered for you.*

_____ Crouse started filling out about 20 legal documents.

__1__ February 2009: Unusual small charges appear on Crouse's bank account.

_____ Crouse called his bank immediately.

_____ Crouse opened a new account at a new bank.

_____ Crouse was late paying bills and was charged with late fees, higher interest costs, and penalties.

_____ August 2009: Big charges began to appear on Crouse's bank account.

_____ Crouse's son left school.

_____ One day Crouse filled out a legal document about a charge, and the next day the bank had accepted similar charges approaching $4,000.

_____ The next day both of Crouse's accounts received a $1,100 charge.

_____ Crouse's identity is still being used in attempts to open credit cards and bank accounts.

C. *When you write about causes and effects, it is important to make cause-effect relationships clear. Read the following sentences. Circle the cause and underline the effect. (Remember, the cause does not always come first.) The first one is done for you.*

1. (The more you transact) the more you're at risk.

2. Those most likely to miss fraud are usually 18 to 24 years old, simply because they

   don't pay enough attention to their accounts.

3. The odds have never been higher for becoming a fraud victim because it's an easy

   crime to perpetrate.

4. In 2008, identity theft resulted in $54 billion in losses to consumers.

5. As a result of unusual activity in his bank account, Crouse called his

   bank immediately.

D. *Write sentences showing either the time or the cause-effect relationships between some of the events in Crouse's life.*

Examples:

Time: After Crouse noticed small charges on his bank account, the charges suddenly got larger.

Cause-Effect: Because his attempts to save his finances have used up all Crouse's savings and retirement accounts, his son left school.

1. _____

_____

2. _____

_____

3. _____

_____

4. _____

_____

E. In "Identity fraud nightmare: One man's story," you read about many kinds of people who are affected by the crime of identity theft.

Circle the types of people you think are most at risk for identity theft. Then underline those types who are least at risk. With a partner, discuss the reasons for your choices. When you answer the question "Why?" you are discussing causes.

bankers	doctors	lawyers	people with computers
children	hackers	movie stars	people without computers
college students	Internet gamblers	older people	shoppers

F. The crime of identity theft is increasing in today's world. Do you know of another type of crime that is also increasing?

Write a paragraph about another type of crime you think is growing and include the reasons for its growth. If you know someone who has been a victim of the crime, briefly tell that person's story.

_____

_____

_____

_____

_____

_____

_____

Writing a Cause-Effect Essay

In this unit, you are going to write an essay that analyzes the causes and effects of a type of crime in your neighborhood, town, or society. When you analyze something, you examine all the parts of it carefully, in order to understand it. When you analyze the causes and effects of a type of crime, you help your reader understand its impact on individuals and society as a whole. You can focus your essay either on the causes or on the effects.

The Cause-Effect Essay

▶ Introduction
▶ Body
▶ Conclusion

Like all essays, a cause-effect essay has three parts.

Step 1   Prewriting

For a cause-effect essay, the prewriting step involves selecting an issue that has clear causes and effects and deciding whether you want to focus on the causes or on the effects. It also involves brainstorming ideas to develop specific points of cause and effect.

Your Own Writing

Choosing Your Assignment

A. *Choose Assignment 1 or Assignment 2.*

1. Identify a problem that your neighborhood, town, or society is having with a certain type of crime. Discuss the causes of this crime. Consider economic causes, such as unemployment, as well as social causes, such as an inadequate police force.

2. Identify a problem that your neighborhood, town, or society is having with a certain type of crime. Discuss the effects of this crime. Consider the effects on institutions, such as schools, as well as the effects on individuals.

B. *Freewrite for 10 minutes on your assignment. Here are some questions to get you started:*

- What do you already know about the type of crime?

- Why is this crime interesting to you?

- What more do you want to find out about your topic?

C. Checking in. *Work with a partner who chose the same assignment. Discuss the ideas you wrote. Did your partner . . .*

- discuss a particular type of crime?

- discuss some possible causes and effects of the crime?

Share your point of view on your partner's topic. Based on your discussion, make changes and additions to your writing.

D. *Complete the brainstorming map. Fill in as much information as you can. You will have a chance to review, change, or add information later in the unit.*

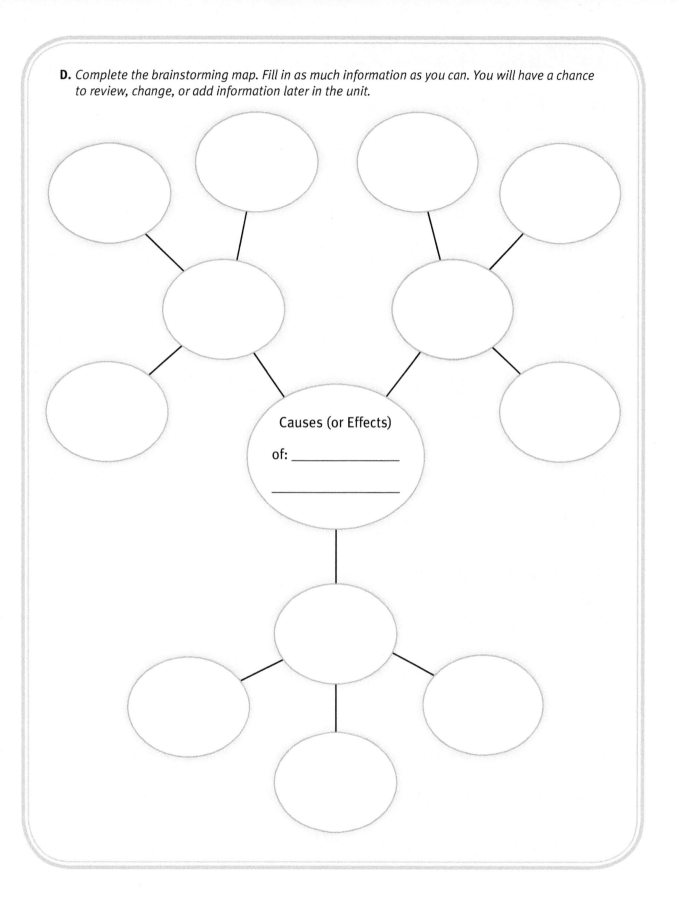

Causes (or Effects)

of: _____

_____

■THE INTRODUCTION

You have practiced two opening strategies for essays, using:

- an interesting or surprising fact

- a thoughtful question

Another effective way to open an essay is to use an interesting example.

You have also learned that the introductory paragraph in an essay gives background information to help the reader understand the thesis statement. (To review the elements of an introductory paragraph, look back at Unit 1, pages 8–9.) In a cause-effect essay, you will first need to decide whether you will focus on causes or on effects.

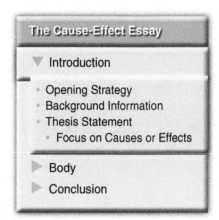

The background information in the introduction of a cause-effect essay focuses on either causes or effects, the opposite of the focus of the body of the essay.

Essay Focus on Causes → Summarize effects in the introduction.

Before reading about the causes of a crime or other phenomenon, your reader will want to know why it is important. A brief summary of the effects in the introduction establishes the importance of the analysis of the causes.

Essay Focus on Effects → Summarize causes in the introduction.

Before reading about the effects of a crime or other phenomenon, your reader will want to know what has caused this to happen. A brief summary of the causes is a good way to introduce the analysis of effects.

A successful thesis statement for a cause-effect essay . . .

- presents the controlling idea of the entire essay, focusing on either causes or effects.

- responds to the assignment.

- contains an idea the writer will develop and support.

- does more than state a fact. It usually presents an arguable assertion or claim.

Focused Practice

A. *Read the essay assignment and sample thesis statements. Decide what the focus of the essay is and what information would be best to include in the introductory paragraph for each thesis statement. Check (✓) the correct answer.*

Identity theft is a growing problem in our society. Discuss either the causes or the effects of this crime.

1. **Thesis Statement:** The current rise in identity theft is caused by several technological and social changes in our society.

   Essay Focus: ＿＿＿ Causes ＿＿＿ Effects

   Summary in the introduction: ＿＿＿ Causes ＿＿＿ Effects

2. Thesis Statement: The crime of identity theft has many negative effects on individuals and society.

Essay Focus: _____ Causes _____ Effects

Summary in the Introduction: _____ Causes _____ Effects

B. *Decide whether the following information would be best for an introduction to an essay based on Thesis Statement 1 (page 98) or on Thesis Statement 2 above. Write 1 or 2.*

- Summarize effects in the introduction if the essay focuses on causes.
- Summarize causes in the introduction if the essay focuses on effects.

_1_ personal bankruptcy for many people

_____ growing concern about privacy of information

_____ the current economic recession

_____ the expansion of the Internet

_____ the number of identity theft victims last year

_____ the growth of Internet security companies

_____ the invention of malware

_____ growing distrust of other people

_____ the amount of money lost by identity theft victims last year

C. *Check (✓) the sentences that would make a good thesis statement for the essay assignment in Exercise A. Explain your choices to a partner.*

_✓_ **1.** The current rise in identity theft is the result of several technological and social changes in our society.

_____ **2.** The crime of identity theft has many negative effects on individuals and society.

_____ **3.** The crime of identity theft cost victims $54 billion last year.

_____ **4.** The current economic recession has resulted in increased crime of many kinds.

_____ **5.** The growing technological sophistication of criminals is causing a rise in identity theft.

_____ **6.** Should we learn to protect ourselves from identity theft?

_____ **7.** Fear of identity theft is changing the ways we live and do business.

_____ **8.** My Aunt Mary's identity was stolen last year.

D. *Read the introduction for an essay on the assignment in Exercise A. Discuss the questions with a partner.*

> When thieves stole Dave Crouse's identity, it ended up costing him $100,000 and his peace of mind. Why is this crime on the rise? At the same time that problems in the international economy are leading more people toward lives of crime, the growth of the Internet is leading us to transact more and more of our business electronically. We love the convenience of banking and shopping online, but it can leave a trail that thieves from all over the world can follow. The people who assume our identities hack into our accounts, steal as much as they can, and then rack up more charges, spreading fear. It is clear that the crime of identity theft has many negative effects on individuals and society.

1. What interesting example did the writer use to open the essay? Circle it.

2. Does the background information focus on causes or effects? Check (✔) the sentence that presents this background information.

3. Underline the thesis statement. Does it focus on causes or effects?

4. What ideas in the thesis statement will be developed in the essay? Double underline them.

Your Own Writing

Finding Out More

A. *Learn more about the essay assignment you chose on page 96. Online or at the library, find as much information as possible about the kind of crime you are analyzing. Research these and other questions:*

- How many people are victims of this crime every year? Is this number growing?

- How much money does this crime cost every year?

- Which social conditions may be causing this crime? Is there evidence of this connection?

- How does this crime change people's lives? Are neighbors affected by the crime in addition to the actual victims?

You may want to use the following keywords when you search for information online: type of crime (for example, *burglary*), *victims*, *costs*, *causes*, *location* (for example, *New York City*).

B. *Take notes on what you found out. For example:*

- Record key information about the crime.
- Be sure to note the sources for your information.
- Add relevant information to the brainstorming map on page 97.

Use this information when you write your essay.

C. **Checking in.** *Share your information with a partner, and give each other feedback. Did your partner . . .*

- gather enough facts and details about the crime?
- use at least three reliable sources?

Planning Your Introduction

A. *Write the interesting example you will use for your essay opener.*

_____

_____

B. *List the background information (effects for Assignment 1 or causes for Assignment 2) you will need to include in your introduction.*

_____

_____

_____

C. *Write a draft of your thesis statement. Make sure your thesis statement clearly states either the causes (for Assignment 1) or the effects (for Assignment 2) of a type of crime. Look back at your freewriting and brainstorming map to help you.*

_____

_____

D. **Checking in.** *Discuss your thesis statement with a partner. Did your partner . . .*

- identify the type of crime?
- specify the location (neighborhood, town, city) or society as a whole?
- focus the thesis statement clearly on either causes or effects?

Tell your partner what kind of supporting evidence you expect to see in his or her essay, based on the thesis statement. Based on your partner's feedback, you may want to rewrite your thesis statement.

◼THE BODY

In the body paragraphs of a cause-effect essay, it is important to

- make the analysis of the causes or effects as clear and complete as possible; illustrate these causes or effects with specific descriptions, facts, and examples.

- organize the causes or effects into categories rather than listing several minor, unrelated causes or effects.

- use words and phrases that clearly express cause-and-effect relationships.

You will need at least two body paragraphs in your essay. Here are examples of two ways that you can structure your cause-effect essay.

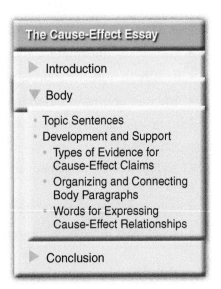

The Cause-Effect Essay
▷ Introduction
▽ Body
 • Topic Sentences
 • Development and Support
  • Types of Evidence for Cause-Effect Claims
  • Organizing and Connecting Body Paragraphs
  • Words for Expressing Cause-Effect Relationships
▷ Conclusion

Examples:

Focus on Causes

Introduction

    Background information on effects

    Thesis statement on causes

Body Paragraph 1: Cause 1

Body Paragraph 2: Cause 2

Body Paragraph 3: Cause 3 (Optional)

Conclusion

Focus on Effects

Introduction

    Background information on causes

    Thesis statement on effects

Body Paragraph 1: Effect 1

Body Paragraph 2: Effect 2

Body Paragraph 3: Effect 3 (Optional)

Conclusion

Developing Body Paragraphs

In a cause-effect essay, it is important to support your claims of cause-effect relationships with as much evidence as possible. Here are some examples of types of evidence for cause-effect claims.

Examples:

Facts: Those most likely to miss fraud are usually 18 to 24 years old.

Statistics: That figure is up 12 percent over 2008 and is 37 percent ahead of 2007.

Statements from Authorities: Identity thieves steal mostly through two means, according to Michael Stanfield, chief executive of Intersections Inc., a risk-management firm.

Examples and Personal Stories: In fewer than six months, some $900,000 in merchandise, gambling and telephone-services were charged to Crouse's debit card.

When you read the body paragraphs on page 103, you will see the difference between weak and strong supporting evidence.

Weak Support

> The crime of identity theft is growing because of the increased use of the Internet for financial transactions. Just six months ago, my aunt, who can't drive anymore, bought her first computer. I thought it would be convenient for her to do her shopping and banking at home, so I set up accounts for her. Unfortunately, Aunt Mary didn't know how to protect her privacy on the Internet, and soon her credit card was being used for mysterious purchases all over the country.

The evidence in this paragraph is weak because it is only one personal example that doesn't prove the claim that identity theft is growing because of the Internet.

Stronger Support

> The crime of identity theft is growing because of the increased use of the Internet for financial transactions. Most personal banking is now conducted on the Internet, providing a rich resource for those who know how to illegally hack into accounts. "The odds have never been higher for becoming a fraud victim," said James Van Dyke, of Javelin Research. The most likely victims are those who don't know or don't bother to protect their information. Just six months ago, my aunt, who can't drive anymore, bought her first computer. I thought it would be convenient for her to do her shopping and banking at home, so I set up accounts for her. Unfortunately, Aunt Mary didn't know how to protect her privacy on the Internet, and soon her credit card was being used for mysterious purchases all over the country.

The evidence in this paragraph is stronger because it includes facts and a statement from an authority. The personal example is now introduced by a sentence that explains its connection to the claim.

Focused Practice

A. *Reread the paragraph on page 103 that provides stronger support.*

1. Underline the facts and statement from an authority.

2. Circle the sentence that explains the connection of the personal example to the claim that identity theft is growing because of the Internet.

B. *In "Identity fraud nightmare" (pages 92–93), find evidence in support of the following claim. Circle the evidence in the reading and label it by type:* facts/statistics, authority, *or* personal story. *Then fill in examples of each type of evidence on the chart below.*

Claim: Identity theft can cause severe problems for the victims.

Types of Evidence	Examples from Reading
Facts and Statistics	Example 1: Example 2:
Authority	Name of Person: Statement:
Personal Story	Name of Person: Summary of Story:

Organizing and Connecting Body Paragraphs

As you explore the crime you are writing about, you may discover some minor causes or effects. First, create a list of the causes or effects you want to include in your essay. Then group the causes or effects into paragraphs rather than writing several short paragraphs discussing a single cause or effect.

Next, decide on the order of your paragraphs. There are a number of ways to order paragraphs:

- Chronological order works well when the *time order* of the causes or effects is important.

  For example, in an essay about the causes of identity theft, you might write first about the technological changes that made the crime possible and then about the subsequent economic problems that pushed people into a life of crime.

- Order of importance generally moves from the *least important* cause or effect to the *most important*, ending the essay with its strongest point.

  For example, if you are discussing the crime of illegal graffiti (spray-painting gang signs on buildings), you might begin by discussing the unattractiveness of graffiti and the cost of its removal and save your most important effect for the last body paragraph: the research showing that high levels of graffiti (and other property destruction) often encourage more serious crimes to increase in a neighborhood.

- Order of specificity moves from the *specific* (particular) to the *general*. This organization works well when something affects individual victims and, through them, affects society as a whole.

  For example, in an essay on the effects of the crime of identity theft, it might be most effective to move from the particular effects on the individual victim to the general effects on technology and society.

You can show the organization of your essay in the sentences that begin and connect your paragraphs.

Examples:

Chronological Order: After the technological changes that made identity theft easier, the subsequent economic downturn pushed more people to use the new technology in a life of crime.

Order of Importance: Even more serious than the unattractiveness and cost of illegal graffiti is its tendency to increase levels of more serious crime in a neighborhood.

Order of Specificity (moving from specific effects on individuals to more general effects on society): Can all these attacks on your computer be avoided by careful attention to Internet security? Probably not, but Internet security is becoming big business. (Note the technique of beginning a paragraph with a question connecting to the previous paragraph.)

Focused Practice

A. *Work with a partner. Look at the following topic and list of minor effects, which the writer grouped into three categories. The numbers indicate each category.*

Topic: Effects of the crime of identity theft

1 unexpected credit card charges

1 depression

2 necessity to buy Internet security

1 marital and family problems

1 empty bank accounts

3 growing social distrust

3 distrust of technology

1 bankruptcy

1 bad credit scores

2 necessity to encrypt all information

B. *Read and analyze the writer's outlines and body paragraphs; they are based on the categories in Exercise A (page 105).*

- Find and underline the information from the outlines in the body paragraphs.
- Check (✓) each item as you find it. The first one is done for you.

Body Paragraph 1: Effects on individuals

a. financial effects

   ✓   empty bank accounts

_____ unexpected credit card charges

_____ bankruptcy

_____ bad credit scores

b. psychological effects

_____ depression

_____ marital and family problems

The immediate effects on the victim are financial, and they only grow worse. In 2009, 1.1 million Americans lost $57 billion to identity theft, and the losses are growing every year. Victims typically find that their <u>bank accounts, sometimes even retirement accounts, have been completely or partially emptied.</u> Their credit cards have multiple charges, often delivered to different addresses around the country and the world, so it is difficult to trace the identity of the thieves. In less than six months Crouse had $900,000 in mysterious charges on his credit cards. When these bills go unpaid, the victim's credit score, which is important for borrowing money or renting an apartment, is often lowered to a dangerous level. Some victims have even had to declare bankruptcy. The random misfortune of identity theft can result in psychological problems such as depression or cause marital and family problems.

Body Paragraph 2: Effects on the use of technology

_____ **a.** necessity to buy Internet security   _____ **b.** necessity to encrypt all information

---

Can all these problems be avoided by careful attention to Internet security? Probably not, but Internet security is becoming big business. Symantec, the largest manufacturer of security software, saw record profits in recent years. Even though antivirus software can slow down older computers, many people tolerate the inconvenience. They are afraid of computer invaders, such as keystroke malware that can copy all of a user's keystrokes, including account numbers and passwords. Most sensitive information is encrypted before it is sent over wireless networks, but the fear now is that even encryption won't stop the thievery. According to the Wireless Safety website, "This can only provide enough security to make a hacker's job more difficult."

Body Paragraph 3: Effects on society

_____ **a.** distrust of technology　　　_____ **b.** growing social distrust

The technical costs of identity theft are accompanied by growing social costs. The Internet brings people around the world together in many ways, with Skype calls and large international Internet retailers such as Amazon. But now it has also made people feel vulnerable to attacks from around the world. Some older citizens are too fearful to use the Internet. My mother, for example, who received a series of virus-infected spam after she did some Internet shopping, has given up using the Internet and advises me to do the same. This is regrettable because the elderly, with their limited mobility, could benefit greatly from in-home shopping and banking. Some of the elderly may begin to feel even more separated from a highly technical society.

C. _Work with a partner to organize the following minor causes into body paragraphs. Group the list of causes into the three categories as shown in the outline on page 108. Then write them in the outline. The first item has been done for you._

Topic: Causes of a college canceling the women's basketball team

__1__ The basketball budget can only support one team.

_____ The team was caught cheating.

_____ The men's basketball team sells more tickets.

_____ A small number of women tried out for the team.

_____ The women's gym has been turned into a soccer field.

_____ The women's basketball star graduated last year.

_____ Alumni donate more money to men's basketball.

_____ Other colleges in the area have canceled women's basketball.

_____ Sports travel has grown more expensive.

1. Financial causes

   a. _The basketball budget can only support one team._

   b. _____

   c. _____

   d. _____

2. Lack of interest within the community

   a. _____

   b. _____

   c. _____

3. Problems with the team

   a. _____

   b. _____

D. *Now (based on the outline in Exercise C above) arrange the paragraphs in the order of importance, from least important to most important so that your essay ends with your most important point. Discuss your choices with your partner. If your answers are different, explain your decisions.*

   a. Least important cause: _____

   b. More important cause: _____

   c. Most important cause: _____

E. *Write sentences connecting the ideas in the body paragraphs that you outlined and arranged in Exercises C and D.*

   a. First sentence in body paragraph 2: _____

   _____

   _____

   b. First sentence in body paragraph 3: _____

   _____

   _____

F. *Work with a partner to organize the following minor effects into body paragraphs. Group the list of effects into the three categories as shown in the outline below. Then write them in the outline. The first item has been done for you.*

Topic: Effects of a college canceling the women's basketball team

_2_ The players will be disappointed.

_____ The college will have more money for other sports and activities.

_____ The distribution of the sports money will be unfair to women.

_____ Young female athletes might choose other colleges.

_____ Men's basketball games might become more popular.

_____ Young women will have fewer athletic role models.

_____ The college will violate Title IX, a law that requires equality for men's and women's college sports.

1. Effects on college sports

    a. _____

    b. _____

2. Ethical (moral) effects

    a. *The players will be disappointed.* _____

    b. _____

    c. _____

3. Financial effects

    a. _____

    b. _____

G. *Now (based on Exercise F) arrange the paragraphs in the order of importance, from least important to most important. Add the categories* **effects on college sports, ethical effects,** *and* **financial effects** *in a logical order below. Discuss your choices with your partner.*

    a. Least important effect: _____

    b. More important effect: _____

    c. Most important effect: _____

H. *Write sentences connecting the ideas in the body paragraphs that you outlined and arranged in Exercises F and G (page 109).*

a. First sentence in body paragraph 2

_____

_____

b. First sentence in body paragraph 3

_____

_____

Words for Expressing Cause-and-Effect Relationships

The English language has many ways of showing cause-and-effect relationships.

Verbs that Introduce a Cause		
The drop in attendance	**was caused by**	the high ticket prices.
Many bad feelings	**will result from**	the cancellation.
The sports budget	**is affected by**	alumni donations.

Verbs that Introduce an Effect		
The star player's graduation	**caused**	the team to lose focus.
The high cost of travel	**has resulted in**	the cancellation of many games.
The cancellation	**has made**	the players depressed.

Subordinating Conjunctions		
The school was fined	**since**	the players cheated.
Female athletes are choosing other schools	**because**	the college canceled women's basketball.

Introductory Adverbs		
There is no women's basketball.	**Therefore,**	men's basketball is becoming more popular.
Women's basketball didn't attract enough fans.	**Consequently,**	it was canceled.
Sports are important for all the students.	**For this reason,**	the college should consider another sport for women.
Women's sports are usually not as popular.	**Thus,**	they are more easily canceled.

Prepositional Phrases	
As a result of the budget problems,	the college has canceled several programs.
Because of the laws on fairness in college sports,	the college will need to consider another sport for women.

Focused Practice

A. *Write five cause-and-effect statements, combining the phrases from the chart below and on page 110. The first one is done for you.*

Causes	Effects
a suspicious credit card charge	an increase in crime
malware attack	checking the bank account
economic recession	keystrokes recorded
the Internet	inability to pay bills
loss of savings	increased access to bank account

1. *a suspicious credit card charge/checking the bank account*

   Because of a suspicious credit card charge, I checked my bank account.

2. _____

   _____

3. _____

   _____

4. _____

   _____

5. _____

   _____

6. _____

   _____

B. *Review the chart on page 110. Then complete the paragraph by adding words that show cause and effect. Pay attention to grammar and punctuation.*

> The more business you transact on the Internet, the more you are at
>
> risk _____ you leave a trail behind. Most identity theft
> ⎯⎯ 1.
>
> _____ malware that is secretly installed on your computer.
> ⎯⎯ 2.
>
> _____ the malware can track all your key strokes, it records
> ⎯⎯ 3.
>
> your account numbers and passwords. Criminals use this information to
>
> make charges on your credit cards or withdrawals from your bank accounts.
>
> *(continued)*

_____ the danger of identity theft, many people are now
4.

more conscious of the need for Internet security. The growth of companies such

as Symantec _____ the dangers of malware, spyware, and
5.

Trojan horses. _____, the crime of identity theft ends up being
6.

expensive for all of us, not only the immediate victims.

C. *Write sentences related to your writing assignment, either Assignment 1 or Assignment 2. Include the following cause-and-effect language. You might use some of these sentences in your essay.*

1. Verbs that introduce a cause

_____

_____

2. Verbs that introduce an effect

_____

_____

3. Subordinating conjunctions

_____

_____

4. Introductory adverbs

_____

_____

5. Prepositional phrases

_____

_____

Your Own Writing

Planning Your Body Paragraphs

A. *Your essay will focus on causes or effects. Before you begin writing your body paragraphs, complete the outline below.*

- Copy your thesis statement from page 101.

- Review the ways to organize a cause-effect essay on page 102.

- If you want to experiment with more than one method of organization, complete additional outlines on a separate sheet of paper.

Cause-Effect Essay

▷ Thesis Statement: _____

_____

▷ Body Paragraph 1

   ▷ Topic Sentence: _____

   _____

      ▷ Cause or Effect 1: Supporting Details:

- _____

- _____

- _____

▷ Body Paragraph 2

   ▷ Topic Sentence: _____

   _____

      ▷ Cause or Effect 2: Supporting Details:

- _____

- _____

- _____

▸ Body Paragraph 3 (Optional)

　　▸ Topic Sentence: _____

　　　_____

　　　▸ Cause or Effect 3: Supporting Details:

　　　　• _____

　　　　• _____

　　　　• _____

B. Checking in. *Share your outline with a partner. Did your partner . . .*

- provide enough supporting details?
- organize his or her essay in
  - chronological order?
  - specific to general order?
  - least important to most important order?

Based on your partner's feedback, you may want to rewrite parts of your outline.

▮ THE CONCLUSION

A cause-effect essay needs to leave the reader with a sense that the issue and the writer's cause-effect analysis are important. You have learned several strategies for concluding an essay, including

- looking to the future
- a call to action

In a cause-effect essay, you can use these or other strategies to leave your readers with a clear sense of your cause-effect analysis and its significance to the reader and society.

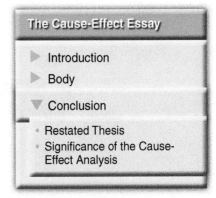

In your conclusion, return to your thesis statement and brainstorm reasons for the significance of the analysis. Ask yourself why the ideas in your essay are important and make a list of reasons.

Example:

Return to Thesis Statement

With the crime of identity theft growing, it is frightening that any of us could become victims. It is also disheartening to see the ways that this fear affects society as a whole.

Brainstorming List of Reasons

Why are the ideas in my essay important?

- The Internet is becoming more popular all the time, so the crime could continue to grow.
- Other forms of technology could promote crime.
- We don't want a society in which we are all afraid.
- We need to do more to protect ourselves.

Focused Practice

Read the following conclusion to a cause-effect essay. Work with a partner to answer the questions.

> With the crime of identity theft growing, it is frightening that any of us could become victims. It is also disheartening to see the ways that this fear affects the society as a whole. All of us need to do more to protect our information on the Internet, but we also need to pay attention to new forms of technology and the ways they can be exploited by criminals. If we carry all our information and passwords on our smart phones, will this make us vulnerable to forms of theft that weren't possible when the criminals only took our wallets? Because we don't want to live in an atmosphere of fear, we need to consider the weaknesses as well as the strengths of the technology in which we invest.

1. Reread the "Brainstorming List of Reasons" above. Which reasons from the list did the writer choose to use in the conclusion?

_____

_____

_____

2. What action(s) is this writer encouraging the reader to take?

_____

_____

3. What question does the writer ask about the future?

_____

_____

Your Own Writing

Planning Your Conclusion

A. *What will you put in your conclusion? List your ideas here.*

_____

_____

B. *Write the sentence that will remind the reader of your thesis statement.*

_____

_____

C. *What strategy will you use to close the essay?*

_____

_____

D. Checking in. *Share your ideas with a partner. Did your partner . . .*

- make clear the significance of the cause-effect analysis?

- choose an effective strategy?

- discover a new and interesting way to phrase his or her thesis statement?

Writing Your First Draft

A. *Read the* **Tip for Writers.** *Review your notes on pages 97, 101, and 113–114. Then write the first draft of your essay. When you are finished, give your essay a working title.*

> **Tip for Writers**
>
> When you write your first draft, be sure that you state time relationships and cause-effect relationships clearly.

B. *After you write the first draft, put in citations for any sources you used. Use MLA style for citations within and at the end of your essay. See Unit 2 (pages 49–50) and the Appendix on pages 194–195 for more information on MLA style.*

C. *Hand in your draft to your teacher.*

Revising your work is an essential part of the writing process. This is your opportunity to be sure that your essay has all the important pieces and that it is clear.

Focused Practice

A. *You have read parts of this cause-and-effect essay already. Now read the entire essay to see how the parts fit together*

Identify Theft

When thieves stole Dave Crouse's identity, it ended up costing him $100,000 and his peace of mind (Waters). Why is this crime on the rise? As problems in the international economy are leading more people toward lives of crime, the growth of the Internet is leading us to transact more and more of our business electronically. We love the convenience of banking and shopping online, but it can leave a trail that thieves from all over the world can follow. The people who assume our identities hack into our accounts, steal as much as they can, and then rack up more charges, spreading fear. It is clear that the crime of identity theft has many negative effects on individuals and society.

The immediate effects on the victim are financial, and they only grow worse. In 2009, 1.1 million Americans lost $57 billion to identity theft, and the losses are growing every year. Victims typically find that their bank accounts, sometimes even retirement accounts, have been completely or partially emptied. Their credit cards have multiple charges, often delivered to different addresses around the country and the world, so it is difficult to trace the identity of the thieves. In less than six months Crouse had $900,000 in mysterious charges on his credit cards (Waters). When these bills go unpaid, the victim's credit score, which is important for borrowing money or renting an apartment, is often lowered to a dangerous level. Some victims have even had to declare bankruptcy. The random misfortune of identity theft can result in psychological problems such as depression or cause marital and family problems.

Can all these problems be avoided by careful attention to Internet security? Probably not, but Internet security is becoming big business. Symantec, the largest manufacturer of security software, saw record profits in recent years (Madway). Even though antivirus software can slow down older computers, many people tolerate the inconvenience. They are afraid of computer invaders, such as keystroke

(continued)

---

malware that can copy all of a user's keystrokes, including account numbers and passwords. Most sensitive information is now encrypted before it is sent over wireless networks, but the fear is that even encryption won't stop the thievery. According to the Wireless Safety website (wirelesssafety.org), "This can only provide enough security to make a hacker's job more difficult."

The technical costs of identity theft are accompanied by growing social costs. The Internet brings people around the world together in many ways, with Skype calls and large international Internet retailers such as Amazon. But now it has also made people feel vulnerable to attacks from around the world. Some older citizens are too fearful to use the Internet. My mother, for example, who received a series of virus-infected spam after she did some Internet shopping, has given up using the Internet and advises me to do the same. This is regrettable because the elderly, with their limited mobility, could benefit greatly from in-home shopping and banking. Some of the elderly may begin to feel even more separated from a highly technical society.

With the crime of identity theft growing, it is frightening that any of us could become victims. It is also disheartening to see the ways that this fear affects the society as a whole. All of us need to do more to protect our information on the Internet, but we also need to pay attention to new forms of technology and the ways that criminals can use them. If we begin to carry all our information and passwords on our smart phones, will this make us vulnerable to forms of theft that weren't possible when the criminals only took our wallets? Because we don't want to live in an atmosphere of fear, we need to consider the weaknesses as well as the strengths of the technology in which we invest.

Works Cited

Madway, Gabriel. "Symantic profits beats Street, approves buyback." *Reuters.com.* Reuters.com, 27 Jan. 2011. Web. 4 Feb. 2011.

Waters, Jennifer. "Identity fraud nightmare: One man's story." *Marketwatch.com.* MarketWatch, 10 Feb. 2010. Web. 4 Feb. 2011.

Wireless Safety.org. Wireless Safety, 2007. Web. 4 Feb. 2011.

B. *Work with a partner. Answer the questions about the essay.*

1. What is the thesis statement? Underline it.

2. What category of effects is described in paragraph 2? Circle the words that tell you.

3. What category of effects is described in paragraph 3? Circle the words that tell you.

4. What category of effects is described in paragraph 4? Circle the words that tell you.

5. Which paragraph makes a transition from the previous paragraph with a question? Underline the question.

6. Which paragraph makes a transition by mentioning two kinds of effects—those in the previous paragraph and those in the following paragraph? Underline the sentence.

7. Which paragraph do you think presents the strongest support? Check (✓) the paragraph and explain your choice to your partner.

8. Does the conclusion convince you that identity theft is a significant issue? Circle the part of the conclusion that convinces you the most.

C. Checking in. *Discuss your marked-up essays with another pair of students. Then in your group, share what you found most interesting about the essay. Explain your answer.*

Building Word Knowledge

The writer included many job-related collocations in "Identity Theft" including the ones below.

credit score	peace of mind	retirement account
declare bankruptcy	record profits	smart phones

Complete the following conversation with collocations from the box. Then practice the conversation with a partner. There is one extra collocation.

CUSTOMER: Good morning. I'm here to open a _____.
                                                        1.

BANK OFFICER: Good morning. I would be happy to help you with that. Please fill out this

form. As soon as I have your social security number, I can look up your

_____.
        2.

CUSTOMER: I'm afraid I'm a little nervous about giving you my social security

number. Someone used my social security number to hack into my

checking account and steal my money last year. I almost had to

_____.
        3.

BANK OFFICER: I understand, sir. I can assure you that this institution will not disclose

your personal financial information to any other party. You can maintain

your _____.
            4.

(continued)

CUSTOMER: Well, OK, then, here is my information.

BANK OFFICER: Thank you, sir. We hope you are pleased with your new account and will invest in more financial products with us in the future. Our investments are showing _____.

5.

Your Own Writing

Revising Your Draft

A. *Reread the first draft of your essay. Use the Revision Checklist to identify parts of your writing that might need improvement.*

B. *Review your plans and notes, and your responses to the Revision Checklist. Then revise your first draft. Save your revised essay. You will look at it again in the next section.*

Revision Checklist

Did you . . .

☐ express the controlling idea of the essay in your thesis statement?

☐ give enough background information in your introduction?

☐ clearly state time and cause-effect relationships?

☐ focus each body paragraph on a cause or effect?

☐ give enough details, such as facts and examples, to support and develop your controlling ideas?

☐ restate the controlling idea of the essay in your conclusion?

☐ connect the parts of your essay?

☐ use an effective concluding strategy?

☐ use any collocations in your essay?

☐ give your essay a good title?

☐ cite any sources that you used in your essay?

■ GRAMMAR PRESENTATION

Before you hand in your revised essay, you must check it for any errors in grammar, punctuation, and spelling. In this section, you will learn about the passive voice. You will focus on this grammar when you edit and proofread your essay.

Passive Voice

Grammar Notes	Examples
1. A sentence in the **passive voice** has a corresponding sentence in the **active voice**. The object in the active sentence becomes the subject in the passive sentence. We can say that the subject of a passive sentence is acted upon.	object • The police solved **the crime**. subject • **The crime** was solved quickly.
The subject of the active sentence becomes the agent (preceded by the preposition **by**) in the passive sentence or disappears.	subject • **Someone stole** the credit card numbers. agent • They **were stolen (by someone)**.
Be Careful! Don't overuse the passive voice in writing. Use the passive voice when you want to emphasize that a subject is acted upon.	
2. Passive sentences are formed with *be* + past participle. They occur in present, past, and future forms.	• Most Internet transactions **are encrypted**. • My bank transaction **was encrypted**. • Your credit card number **will be encrypted**.
Use the passive with a **by** phrase when it is important to mention the agent of the verb.	agent • The merchandise was ordered **by a man in London**.
Use the passive without a **by** phrase when the agent of the verb is unknown or clear from the context.	• In the future, even more business **will be transacted** on the Internet.
3. To form the present passive with a **modal**, use the modal + *be* + past participle.	• Personal information **should be protected**.
To form the past passive with a modal, use the modal + *have been* + past participle.	• Unprotected information **could have been accessed** by hackers.

(continued)

4. Form the **passive causative** with *have* or *get* + object + past participle. Use the passive causative to talk about services or activities that people arrange for someone else to do.

- The thief **had** the address of the account **changed**.

Be Careful! Don't confuse the simple past causative with the past perfect.

- We had our phone number removed from the list. *(simple past causative—someone else deleted our number)*
- We had deleted our phone number from the list. *(past perfect—we did this before a specific time in the past)*

5. Passive sentences with *that* clauses or infinitive phrases are common in academic writing.

- Young people are considered **(to be) the most at risk**.

Be Careful! The construction with *it* occurs only with verbs that can be followed by a clause beginning with *that*.

- **It** is now feared **that even encryption won't stop the criminals**.
  Not: It is now feared ~~how criminals will avoid encryption~~.

Focused Practice

A. *Look at the credit card application form on page 123. Then complete the sentences below. Use the active or passive voice and the correct form of the verb in parentheses. For some sentences, more than one answer may be possible.*

1. The application form _____ the applicant's current address.
   (require)

2. The name of a relative _____.
   (request)

3. The company wants to know if the applicant's residence

   _____.
   (own or rent)

4. All loans, debts, or obligations _____.
   (must report)

5. The company wants to know how long the applicant _____
   (work)

   for his current employer.

6. The application form _____ by the applicant.
   (must sign)

Credit Card Application

Applicant Information		
Name:		
Date of birth:	Country:	Phone:
Current address:		
Own Rent (Please circle)	Monthly payment or rent:	How long?
Name of a relative not residing with you:	Relationship:	Phone:

Employment Information		
Employer:		
Employer address:		How long?
Phone:	Email:	Fax:
Position:	Hourly Salary (Please circle)	Annual income:

Loans, Debts, or Obligations		
Description:	Account no.:	Amount:

I authorize the credit card company to verify the information provided on this form as to my credit and employment history.

Signature of applicant	Date

B. *Use the passive causative to describe the actions of a crime victim. You will need to add an appropriate verb.*

1. _He had his credit card canceled._ _____ (credit card)

2. _____ (locks on his doors)

3. _____ (driver's license)

4. _____ (bank account)

5. _____ (broken window)

C. *Read and edit the paragraph. There are seven mistakes in the use of the passive voice. The first mistake is already corrected. Find and correct six more.*

According to a report from Symantec, the biggest threat on the Internet now comes from botnets.

These collections of computers are also know as *zombie armies* because they have set up by a
~~known~~

master to follow orders. Most are home computers that may be inadequately protect by firewalls

and other safeguards, allowing the master to infect the computer with a Trojan horse that will

activate later. At a certain time, the master will have massive amounts of spam or viruses send by his

zombie army. The attacks can cause system breakdowns if they are directing to a specific target. It is

believe that computers all over the world are vulnerable to these botnet attacks.

D. *Write five sentences related to the topic you chose on page 96. Use the passive voice. These may be sentences you already have in your essay.*

1. _____

_____

2. _____

_____

3. _____

_____

4. _____

_____

5. _____

_____

Your Own Writing

Editing Your Draft

A. *Use the Editing Checklist to edit and proofread your essay.*

B. *Prepare a clean copy of the final draft of your essay and hand it in to your teacher.*

Editing Checklist
Did you . . .
☐ include the passive voice and use it correctly?
☐ use correct verb forms, punctuation, and spelling?
☐ use collocations and other words correctly?

UNIT 5 Problems in Sports

IN THIS UNIT You will be writing an essay about a problem in sports and a possible solution.

Athletes used to win competitions on the basis of skill, training, and teamwork, but now some athletes are taking drugs that can improve their performance. Even though most of these performance-enhancing drugs can cause serious health problems and are illegal, athletes continue to use them. What do you think should be done about the problem of athletes' drug use?

Planning for Writing

■ BRAINSTORM

A. *Some sports in which athletes have been caught using performance-enhancing drugs are bicycle racing, Olympic running, and bodybuilding. Why do you think performance-enhancing drugs are illegal in sports? Discuss your answer with a partner.*

B. Using a *Wh-* Questions Chart. You can use a *wh-* questions chart to gather information for a writing assignment.

Work with a partner. What information do you need in order to learn more about the problem of athletes' drug use? Make a list of questions to ask when you investigate.

Who?	
What?	
When?	
Where?	
Why? *Why do some athletes take illegal performance-enhancing drugs?*	
How?	

C. *With your partner, brainstorm three possible solutions to the problem of drugs in sports.*

1. _____

   _____

2. _____

   _____

3. _____

   _____

■ READ

Read the article about performance-enhancing drugs from an online South African magazine.

Athletes and drugs: an abusive relationship

By VRINDA MAHESHWARI in the *Daily Maverick*, 14 October 2010

1   **The 2010 Commonwealth Games is just the latest sporting event tainted[1] by a doping scandal. Three athletes have tested positive for drugs so far, not counting athletes who tested positive before the Games even began. When will they ever learn? Will they ever learn?**

2   The third positive drug test at the Commonwealth Games occurred on Wednesday. Rani Yadav, an Indian athlete who participated in the women's 20-kilometer (12.4 mile) walk, tested positive for a banned anabolic steroid[2] commonly called nandrolone. The Commonwealth Games Federation court has suspended Yadav until a hearing of the evidence. Use of nandrolone is prohibited by the World Anti-Doping Agency. The provisional suspension has come as a huge disappointment to the host country.

3   Lalit Bhanot, the secretary general of the organizing committee, called the latest incident "unfortunate." He said that the National Anti-Doping Agency had done its best to test athletes, but it was difficult to control doping if sportspeople were dedicated to taking banned substances. Doping has become a recurrent[3] problem in Indian sports, with weightlifting bearing the greatest load: The agency banned six offenders last year and almost as many so far this year. Three swimmers, six wrestlers, and one weightlifter from India have tested positive for the drug methylhexaneaemine in 2010 alone.

4   Of course, drugs and sports have gone hand-in-hand[4] since competitive events began. In ancient Greece, Olympic athletes would eat specially prepared meat (including lizards) and drink magic potions to boost their performances. Whether this actually worked or not is debatable, but there's no denying the intention to cheat was there.

5   It's no different in modern sport, which is rife with[5] suspicions about performance-enhancing drug use by many top athletes. The usual suspects are human-growth hormones (which promote physical development), anabolic steroids (drugs that resemble testosterone and control the metabolic rate), beta-blockers, erythropoietin, stimulants, and diuretics.

---

[1] **tainted:** affected by something dishonest
[2] **anabolic steroids:** drugs that make muscles grow quickly
[3] **recurrent:** repeated
[4] **hand-in-hand:** closely related or happening together
[5] **rife with:** full of something bad

6   However, even more serious than the implications for fairness is the fact that many of these drugs have severe side effects, which are not completely understood even today. They pose genuine health risks, which are ignored by athletes who are determined to win their events at all costs. One athlete who paid with his life was Danish cyclist Enemark Jensen. The 24 year-old man lost consciousness and fell off his bike during the 1960 Olympics in Rome, causing his death. He was found to be under the influence of amphetamines.

7   In fact, professional road cycling has been the sport most plagued by doping allegations.[6] The most persistent have been those around Lance Armstrong, an American who won the challenging Tour de France a record seven times, overcame testicular cancer, and set up a foundation to fight cancer. Armstrong has continually denied using illegal performance-enhancing drugs. He has described himself as "the most tested athlete in the world." A 1999 urine sample showed traces of corticosteroid, but medical certificates showed he used an approved cream for injuries which contained the substance. Between September 2008 and March 2009, Armstrong submitted to 24 unannounced drug tests by various anti-doping authorities. All showed negative for performance-enhancing drugs.

8   Arguably the highest-profile case of all time is that of Canada's Ben Johnson. The Jamaican-born runner enjoyed a world-famous career during most of the 1980s, winning two Olympic bronze medals and a gold. He set consecutive 100-meter world records at the 1987 World Championships and the 1988 Summer Olympics. He was later disqualified for doping and lost the Olympic titles and both records.

9   The International Association of Athletics Federations releases a handbook every year listing all the banned substances. Each athlete is responsible for knowing exactly what is going into his or her body. Certain substances are acceptable outside competitions, but not during them, so athletes need to do their homework. The president of the Commonwealth Games Federation, reacting to the doping instances at the 2010 Commonwealth Games, agrees. He says that there is a need to "increase the educational activities where doping is concerned so that the athletes and their coaches know what is required and how to prevent this kind of disgrace."

10   This highlights another facet[7] of the doping issue: the subsequent shame for the athletes involved. Being stripped of your medals, banned for a certain number of years, losing out on advertising sponsorships, and facing the criticism of your teammates and countrymen seems pretty serious. But judging by the number of athletes who still ignore doping regulations, this doesn't seem enough of a deterrent.[8] Perhaps we should return to how the ancient Greeks shamed cheating athletes. They carved their images onto stone statues that lined the pathway to the Olympic stadium, thus capturing their shame forever.

---

[6] **allegations:** unproven accusations
[7] **facet:** one of several parts of a situation, someone's character, etc.; aspect
[8] **deterrent:** something that stops someone from doing something

Building Word Knowledge

Using Verb + Preposition and Adjective + Preposition Combinations. Many English verbs and adjectives are followed by prepositional phrases. It is important to learn the correct prepositions to put after the verbs and adjectives. Here are some examples of verb + preposition and adjective + preposition combinations from "Athletes and drugs: an abusive relationship."

Examples:

. . . who participated in the women's 20-kilometer walk

. . . if sportspeople were dedicated to taking banned substances

. . . Armstrong submitted to 24 unannounced drug tests

. . . he was disqualified for doping

Find five more verb + preposition or adjective + preposition combinations in the article on pages 128–129. Sometimes other words come between the verb or adjective and the preposition. Write the verbs or adjectives and the prepositions that follow them.

1. _____

2. _____

3. _____

4. _____

5. _____

Focused Practice

A. *Read the* Tip for Writers. *Find evidence in the article on pages 128–129 that supports the following claims. The first one is done for you.*

> ### Tip for Writers
>
> When writers describe a problem, they need to **provide enough evidence** to convince the reader that the problem exists and is serious.

1. Doping has become a recurrent problem in Indian sports.

   The agency banned six offenders last year and almost as many so far this year. Three swimmers, six wrestlers, and one weightlifter from India have tested positive for the drug methylhexaneaemine in 2010 alone.

2. Drugs and sports have gone hand-in-hand since competitive events began.

   _____

   _____

   _____

3. The drugs pose genuine health risks.

   _____

   _____

   _____

4. The highest-profile case of all time is that of Canada's Ben Johnson.

_____

_____

_____

B. *Work with a partner. Discuss the evidence from the article. Answer the following question in two or three sentences.*

Are you convinced that drugs are a problem in sports? Why or why not?

_____

_____

_____

_____

C. *What can you infer (guess) from the last two paragraphs of the article? Work with a partner. Check (✓) all ideas that apply.*

_____ **1.** The athletes suffer serious penalties when they get caught taking illegal drugs.

_____ **2.** The penalties successfully stop the athletes from taking the drugs.

_____ **3.** We should carve images in stone of cheating athletes.

_____ **4.** The author approves of performance-enhancing drugs for athletes.

_____ **5.** The author doesn't approve of performance-enhancing drugs for athletes.

D. *Choose a solution from your brainstorming list on page 127, or a solution from the article. Write a paragraph about why this solution would or would not solve the problem of drugs in sports.*

_____

_____

_____

_____

_____

_____

_____

_____

_____

Writing a Problem-Solution Essay

In this unit, you are going to write an essay describing a problem in sports and proposing one or more solutions. The essay will emphasize your opinion or advice on the best solution to the problem.

Like all essays, a problem-solution essay has three parts.

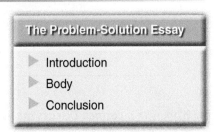

The Problem-Solution Essay

▸ Introduction
▸ Body
▸ Conclusion

Step 1   Prewriting

For a problem-solution essay, prewriting involves finding and selecting a problem you want to write about. It also involves brainstorming possible solutions for the problem and selecting one or more you would like to propose and justify.

Your Own Writing

Choosing Your Assignment

A. *Choose Assignment 1 or Assignment 2.*

1. There are many kinds of problems associated with popular sports. For example, some sports are too dangerous for athletes. Other sports attract unruly fans, creating danger for spectators. Summarize the problem and suggest one or more solutions.

   Here are some suggestions for sports. You can choose one of these or another sport you find interesting.

• baseball	• boxing	• soccer
• basketball	• cricket	• table tennis
• bicycle racing	• running	• tennis

2. Local sports teams and sporting events often encounter problems. For example, the sports stadium may be too old or the team may be having trouble attracting enough spectators. Summarize a problem with a local sports team or sporting event and suggest one or more possible solutions.

B. *Freewrite for 10 minutes on your assignment. Here are some questions to get you started:*

- What do you already know about the topic?

- Why does the topic interest you?

- What personal experience, as a player or a fan, do you have with the problem?

C. Checking in. *Work with a partner who chose the same assignment. Discuss the ideas and details you wrote in Exercise B. Did your partner . . .*

- identify a sports-related problem?
- add information about the sport and the problem?
- describe personal experiences with the sport, team, or event?

Share your point of view on your partner's topic. Based on your discussion, make changes and additions to your writing.

D. *Make a brainstorming map of possible solutions to the problem you chose. In the middle circle, write the problem (for example, drugs in sports). In the outer circles, write possible solutions. You will have a chance to review, change, or add information later in the unit.*

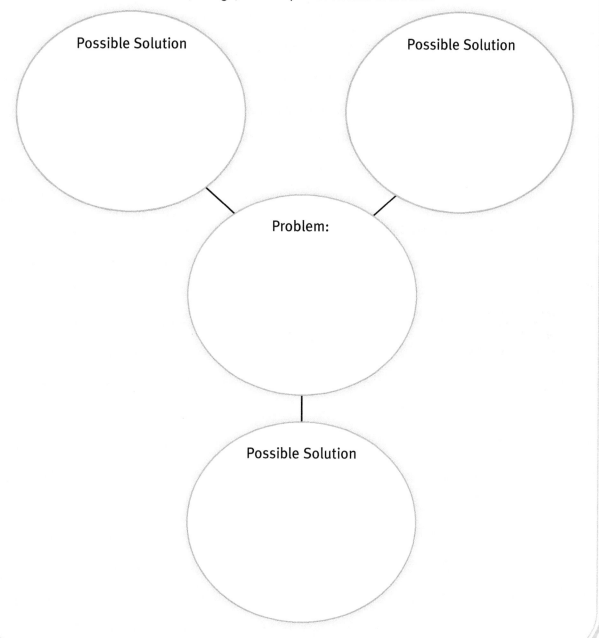

Possible Solution

Possible Solution

Problem:

Possible Solution

■ THE INTRODUCTION

In Unit 1, you learned that the introductory paragraph in an essay gives important background information to help the reader understand the thesis statement.

In a problem-solution essay, the introduction usually provides background information about the subject and introduces the problem. The thesis statement briefly states the problem and solution(s). It may be one or two sentences.

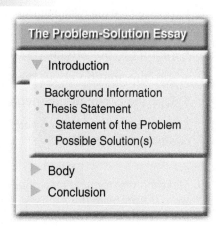

The Problem-Solution Essay

▼ Introduction
 • Background Information
 • Thesis Statement
    • Statement of the Problem
    • Possible Solution(s)

▶ Body
▶ Conclusion

Focused Practice

A. *Read the following essay assignment. Then decide which information you might use as background information for an introductory paragraph on the topic. Check (✓) the sentences you choose and discuss your choices with a partner.*

- Ask yourself this question to help you: *Is this information important?*

- Give reasons for your choices when you and your partner have different opinions.

Performance-enhancing drugs have become a big problem in sporting events all over the world. Summarize the problem and suggest one or more solutions.

_____ **1.** The most common drugs used in weightlifting are corticosteroids.

_____ **2.** Performance-enhancing drugs have ruined the careers of several world-famous athletes.

_____ **3.** Both the Olympics and the Commonwealth games have been affected by drugs.

_____ **4.** My favorite athlete would never take performance-enhancing drugs.

_____ **5.** Performance-enhancing drugs should be legal.

_____ **6.** Serious penalties for athletes have not solved the problem.

B. *Reread the essay assignment in Exercise A. Then, for the following thesis statement, decide which ideas will probably be developed in the essay. Check (✓) the sentences you choose and discuss your choices with a partner.*

Thesis Statement: Performance-enhancing drugs can unfairly advantage some athletes and seriously damage their health, so young people and adult athletes need to be educated about the dangers of these substances.

_____ **1.** Many athletes begin using drugs such as steroids at a young age.

_____ **2.** Different sporting events have different penalties for drug use.

_____ **3.** It is useless to ban drugs since athletes use them anyway.

_____ **4.** In some sports such as weightlifting, bodybuilding drugs have become part of the culture.

_____ **5.** Anabolic steroids can damage the liver.

_____ **6.** Marijuana is accepted as a medicine in some parts of the world.

C. *Read the introduction for an essay on the assignment in Exercise A (page 134). Then discuss the questions with a partner.*

> International sporting events provide an opportunity for athletes from around the world to compete in a healthy environment, away from the usual stress of international relations. Events such as the Olympics and the Commonwealth games are popular because the citizens of each country can cheer for their teams in fair contests. However, not all athletes follow the rules; some of them secretly take drugs. These drugs have ruined the careers of several talented athletes, who have disappointed their fans and fellow citizens. Performance-enhancing drugs can unfairly advantage some athletes and seriously damage their health, so young people and adult athletes need to be educated about the dangers of these substances.

1. Which ideas from Exercise A did the writer use as background?

2. Why did the writer omit some ideas but not others?

3. What is the writer's thesis statement? Underline it. Is it one sentence or two?

4. What problem and solution do you expect the essay to cover?

5. Why does the writer begin with two positive statements about the value of international sporting events?

Your Own Writing

Finding Out More

A. *Research your topic online or at the library.*

- If you chose Assignment 1, your essay will be about a problem in sports. You may want to learn more about the sport in general before you concentrate on a specific problem.

  Then find out what kinds of problems exist in the sport. You may want to use the following keywords when you search for information online: name of sport (e.g., *soccer, baseball*) + *danger, injuries, costs, fans, problems, issues*. Adapt the *wh-*questions you wrote on page 127 to gather information about the specific problem you have chosen.

- If you chose Assignment 2, find information about the local team or sporting event. You may want to interview local fans or players and search for information online. To gather information about the sports team or sporting event, adapt the *wh-*questions you wrote for Exercise C on page 127.

B. *Next, choose one of the articles you read to summarize for your essay.*

- If you chose Assignment 1, select an article that deals with a problem in the sport you are writing about. The article should include the most important information about the problem. When you are writing your body paragraphs, you will write a summary of this information.

- If you chose Assignment 2, select an article from a local newspaper that contains information about the sports team or sporting event. When you are writing your body paragraphs, you will write a summary of this information.

C. *Take notes on what you found out. For example:*

- Record key information about various teams and athletes that you read about.

- Note the sources of your information.

- Add relevant information about the problem and its possible solutions to the brainstorming map on page 133.

Use this information when you write your essay.

D. Checking in. *Share your information with a partner and give each other feedback. Did your partner select . . .*

- an article that he or she will summarize later?

- an article with enough information about a problem?

- an interesting problem to write about?

Planning Your Introduction

A. *List the background information you will need to include in your introduction.*

_____

_____

_____

B. *Write a draft of your thesis statement. Make sure your thesis statement clearly states the problem and the solution(s) your essay will propose. Look back at your freewriting and brainstorming map to help you.*

_____

_____

C. Checking in. *Discuss your thesis statement with a partner. Does your partner's thesis statement . . .*

- clearly state the problem?

- clearly state one or more reasonable solutions?

Tell your partner what kind of supporting evidence you expect to see in his or her essay, based on the thesis statement. Based on your partner's feedback, you may want to rewrite your thesis statement.

■ THE BODY

In a problem-solution essay, you begin by convincing your readers that a problem exists and is serious. You then propose one or more solutions. You may need one or more paragraphs for the problem section or the solution section.

For the problem-solution essay in this unit, you will include a one-paragraph summary of an article about a sports-related problem. Then, in one or more paragraphs, you will suggest one or more solutions.

If you only want to propose one solution for the problem, you can organize the body of your essay according to your reasons for supporting the solution.

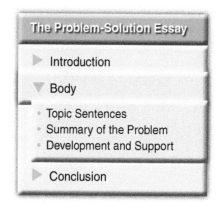

If you want to propose more than one solution for the problem, you can organize the body of your essay according to the various solutions.

Your essay will follow one of the patterns shown below:

Examples:

Multiple Solutions

Introduction + Thesis Statement

Body Paragraph 1: Summary of article describing the problem

Body Paragraph 2: Solution 1

Body Paragraph 3: Solution 2 (more paragraphs, if needed)

Conclusion

One Solution, Multiple Reasons

Introduction + Thesis Statement

Body Paragraph 1: Summary of article describing the problem

Body Paragraph 2: Solution: Reason 1

Body Paragraph 3: Solution: Reason 2 (more paragraphs, if needed)

Conclusion

Summarizing an Article

Summaries, which are common in academic writing, are usually a part of an essay, term paper, or written response in a test. Their purpose is to provide a brief and accurate account of ideas and information from another source or sources. Several principles will help you write effective summaries:

- In your summary of the problem, include only the information and ideas from the source. Do not include additional information or your own opinions.

- Write the summary in complete sentences in paragraph form.

- Include only the most important ideas and information from the source. Do not include secondary supporting details or digressions (writing that is off the subject).

- Paraphrase the language from the source. Do not copy it precisely. (Not every word will require a synonym, however. For example, don't summarize an article on *seatbelts* with the phrase *vehicular restraint devices*. There is no appropriate or necessary synonym for *seatbelt*.)

Focused Practice

A. Finding the Important Ideas and Information. You need to shorten the article to one paragraph, so your first task is to highlight the important ideas that might go into your summary of the article. Don't highlight the supporting details.

Reread the first five paragraphs of the article "Athletes and drugs: An abusive relationship."
Notice that the important ideas are highlighted. Work with a partner to answer the following
questions.

1. Why were these parts of the text highlighted?

2. Why weren't the other parts highlighted?

3. Do you agree that the correct parts have been highlighted? How might you have highlighted this text differently?

Athletes and drugs: an abusive relationship

By VRINDA MAHESHWARI in the *Daily Maverick*, 14 October 2010

1 **The 2010 Commonwealth Games is just the latest sporting event tainted by a doping scandal. Three athletes have tested positive for drugs so far, not counting athletes who tested positive before the Games even began. When will they ever learn? Will they ever learn?**

2 The third positive drug test at the Commonwealth Games occurred on Wednesday. Rani Yadav, an Indian athlete who participated in the women's 20-kilometer (12.4 mile) walk, tested positive for a banned anabolic steroid commonly called nandrolone. The Commonwealth Games Federation court has suspended Yadav until a hearing of the evidence. Use of nandrolone is prohibited by the World Anti-Doping Agency. The provisional suspension has come as a huge disappointment to the host country.

3 Lalit Bhanot, the secretary general of the organizing committee, called the latest incident "unfortunate." He said that the National Anti-Doping Agency had done its best to test athletes, but it was difficult to control doping if sportspeople were dedicated to taking banned substances. Doping has become a recurrent problem in Indian sports, with weightlifting bearing the greatest load: The agency banned six offenders last year and almost as many so far this year. Three swimmers, six wrestlers, and one weightlifter from India have tested positive for the drug methylhexaneaemine in 2010 alone.

4 Of course, drugs and sports have gone hand-in-hand since competitive events began. In ancient Greece, Olympic athletes would eat specially prepared meat (including lizards) and drink magic potions to boost their performances. Whether this actually worked or not is debatable, but there's no denying the intention to cheat was there.

5 It's no different in modern sport, which is rife with suspicions about performance-enhancing drug use by many top athletes. The usual suspects are human-growth hormones (which promote physical development), anabolic steroids (drugs that resemble testosterone and control the metabolic rate), beta-blockers, erythropoietin, stimulants, and diuretics.

6   However, even more serious than the implications for fairness is the fact that many of these drugs have severe side effects, which are not completely understood even today. They pose genuine health risks, which are ignored by athletes who are determined to win their events at all costs. One athlete who paid with his life was Danish cyclist Enemark Jensen. The 24-year-old man lost consciousness and fell off his bike during the 1960 Olympics in Rome, causing his death. He was found to be under the influence of amphetamines.

7   In fact, professional road cycling has been the sport most plagued by doping allegations. The most persistent have been those around Lance Armstrong, an American who won the challenging Tour de France a record seven times, overcame testicular cancer, and set up a foundation to fight cancer. Armstrong has continually denied using illegal performance-enhancing drugs. He has described himself as "the most tested athlete in the world." A 1999 urine sample showed traces of corticosteroid, but medical certificates showed he used an approved cream for injuries which contained the substance. Between September 2008 and March 2009, Armstrong submitted to 24 unannounced drug tests by various anti-doping authorities. All showed negative for performance-enhancing drugs.

8   Arguably the highest-profile case of all time is that of Canada's Ben Johnson. The Jamaican-born runner enjoyed a world-famous career during most of the 1980s, winning two Olympic bronze medals and a gold. He set consecutive 100-meter world records at the 1987 World Championships and the 1988 Summer Olympics. He was later disqualified for doping and lost the Olympic titles and both records.

9   The International Association of Athletics Federations releases a handbook every year listing all the banned substances. Each athlete is responsible for knowing exactly what is going into his or her body. Certain substances are acceptable outside competitions, but not during them, so athletes need to do their homework. The president of the Commonwealth Games Federation, reacting to the doping instances at the 2010 Commonwealth Games, agrees. He says that there is a need to "increase the educational activities where doping is concerned so that the athletes and their coaches know what is required and how to prevent this kind of disgrace."

10   This highlights another facet of the doping issue: the subsequent shame for the athletes involved. Being stripped of your medals, banned for a certain number of years, losing out on advertising sponsorships, and facing the criticism of your teammates and countrymen seems pretty serious. But judging by the number of athletes who still ignore doping regulations, this doesn't seem enough of a deterrent. Perhaps we should return to how the ancient Greeks shamed cheating athletes. They carved their images onto stone statues that lined the pathway to the Olympic stadium, thus capturing their shame forever.

C. Writing the Opening Sentence. *The first sentence of your summary paragraph should include the name of the author, the title of the article, and the main idea of the article.*

Example:

According to Vrinda Maheshwari in "Athletes and drugs: an abusive relationship," the use of performance-enhancing drugs in international sporting events has become a big problem for which there is no clear solution.

The example sentence above follows this common pattern:

According to + the name of the author + *in* + the title of the article + independent clause

Write opening sentences for the article "Athletes and drugs: an abusive relationship" using these other patterns.

1. *In* + the title of the article, the name of the author + reporting verb (*describe, discuss*) + noun phrase.

_____

_____

2. the name of the author + reporting verb (*describe, discuss*) + noun phrase + *in* + the title of the article

_____

_____

D. Writing the Summary Paragraph. *As you summarize the article you chose for your essay, remember not to copy the precise language from the article. Sometimes two (or more) sentences in the article can become one sentence in your summary.*

Example:

Sentences from an Article: The 2010 Commonwealth Games is just the latest sporting event tainted by a doping scandal . . . When will they ever learn? Will they ever learn?

Possible Summary Sentence: The drug allegations at the 2010 Commonwealth Games have led Maheshwari to wonder if the athletes will ever stop using drugs.

Write one summary sentence for each of these sentences or groups of sentences from "Athletes and drugs: an abusive relationship." Try to use as few words as possible. Share your summary sentences with a partner.

1. He said that the National Anti-Doping Agency had done its best to test athletes, but it was difficult to control doping if sportspeople were dedicated to taking banned substances. Doping has become a recurrent problem in Indian sports . . .

_____

_____

2. Of course, drugs and sports have gone hand-in-hand since competitive events began.

_____

_____

(continued)

3. This highlights another facet of the doping issue: the subsequent shame for the athletes involved. Being stripped of your medals, banned for a certain number of years, losing out on advertising sponsorships, and facing the criticism of your teammates and countrymen seems pretty serious. But judging by the number of athletes who still ignore doping regulations, this doesn't seem enough of a deterrent.

_____

_____

Developing Body Paragraphs

In a problem-solution essay, you need to offer one or more reasonable, realistic solutions to the problem. Remember that in order to convince your reader that you have the best solution for the problem, you need to provide enough reasons and evidence to support your solution.

You may also want to discuss other solutions that have not worked in the past or show why your solution is better than other possible solutions.

Focused Practice

A. *On page 135, you read an introductory paragraph for a problem-solution essay. Study the writer's thesis statement and the outline below. Then select reasons and evidence from the list on page 143 and add them to either paragraph 2 or 3, as appropriate. Discuss your choices with a partner. The first one is done for you.*

Thesis Statement: Performance-enhancing drugs can unfairly advantage some athletes and damage their health, so young people and adult athletes need to be educated about the dangers of these substances.

Body Paragraph 1: Summary of "Athletes and drugs: an abusive relationship" (the problem)

Body Paragraph 2: Solution—Educate young people.

Most athletes begin training at a young age. _____

_____

_____

_____

Body Paragraph 3: Solution—Educate adult athletes.

_____

_____

_____

_____

Reasons and Evidence

1. ~~Most athletes begin training at a young age.~~

2. The rules for permissible drugs vary by event.

3. A lot of misinformation about performance-enhancing drugs is spread over the Internet.

4. The competition among young athletes in training can be fierce.

5. Young people are easily influenced by peers.

6. Researchers are constantly discovering new side effects of drugs.

7. Drug offenses can easily end an athlete's career.

8. Informing athletes of penalties has not solved the problem.

B. *Read the following thesis statement. Then work with a partner to brainstorm reasons and evidence to support the solution.*

Thesis Statement: Performance-enhancing drugs can unfairly advantage some athletes and damage their health. Since current penalties are not effective in ending the practice, more serious penalties should be enforced.

_____

_____

_____

_____

_____

_____

Connecting Body Paragraphs

In Unit 1, you learned that a topic sentence often provides a transition from the controlling idea in the previous body paragraph and states the topic of the following paragraph. Writers use many transition words and techniques to connect their body paragraphs including the following:

- **continued content** to link ideas
- **adverbial phrases** to set up a logical relationship between paragraphs (*of course, in this way*)
- **introductory adverbs** to set up a logical relationship between paragraphs (*however, moreover*)
- **pronouns** or **adjectives** that refer to ideas presented earlier (*this, it, these*)
- **articles** that indicate continued content (*the, another*)
- **comparisons** (*better, more*)

Focused Practice

A. *Work with a partner. Reread these two body paragraphs from the article "Athletes and drugs: an abusive relationship." Notice in the topic sentence, the highlighted words that connect the two paragraphs. Then discuss the questions below.*

5   It's no different in modern sport, which is rife with suspicions about performance-enhancing drug used by many top athletes. The usual suspects are human-growth hormones (which promote physical development), anabolic steroids (drugs that resemble testosterone and control the metabolic rate), beta-blockers, erythropoietin, stimulants and diuretics.

6   However, even more serious than the implications for fairness is the fact that many of these drugs have severe side effects, which are not completely understood even today. They pose genuine health risks, which are ignored by athletes who are determined to win their events at all costs. One athlete who paid with his life was Danish cyclist Enemark Jensen. The 24-year-old man lost consciousness and fell off his bike during the 1960 Olympics in Rome, causing his death. He was found to be under the influence of amphetamines.

       1. Underline the introductory adverb in the topic sentence. Why do you think the writer used this word?

       2. What phrase links the two paragraphs by setting up a comparison? Circle it.

       3. Which words or phrases in the topic sentence refer to ideas from the previous paragraph? Double underline them.

B. *Read these topic sentences for the body paragraphs in the essay outlined in Exercise A, page 142. Identify the connecting words between paragraphs and the various techniques the writer used. Compare answers with a partner. The first one is done for you.*

Thesis Statement: Performance-enhancing drugs can unfairly advantage some athletes and seriously damage their health, so young people and adult athletes need to be educated about the dangers of these substances.

Body Paragraph 1: Summary of "Athletes and drugs: an abusive relationship" (the problem)

Body Paragraph 2: Solution—Educate young people.

Topic Sentence: The best way to approach this difficult problem is to educate young people about the dangers of performance-enhancing drugs.

    Words that show connection: *this difficult problem*

    Techniques: *demonstrative adjective; repeated content*

Body Paragraph 3: Solution—Educate adult athletes.

Topic Sentence: However, the education campaign can't end with young people because adult athletes need specific information about the drugs, their side effects, and possible penalties.

Words that show connection: _____

Techniques: _____

Your Own Writing

Planning Your Body Paragraphs

A. *You are going to organize your body paragraphs by describing a problem and proposing one or more solutions. Before you begin writing your body paragraphs, complete one of the outlines below.*

- Copy your thesis statement from page 137.

- Review the ways to organize a problem-solution essay on page 138.

- Select the method and number of paragraphs best suited to your problem and solution(s). If you want to experiment with more than one method of organization, complete both outlines.

Problem-Solution Essay

Thesis Statement: _____

_____

Multiple Solutions

▶ Body Paragraph 1: Summary of an Article

  ▶ Topic Sentence: (includes name of the author, title of the article, and main idea of

  the article) _____

  _____

    ▶ Important Information from the Article:

      • _____

      • _____

      • _____

▷ Body Paragraph 2: Solution 1

   ▷ Topic Sentence: _____

     _____

      ▷ Supporting Reasons and Evidence for Solution 1:

        • _____

        • _____

        • _____

▷ Body Paragraph 3: Solution 2

   ▷ Topic Sentence: _____

     _____

      ▷ Supporting Reasons and Evidence for Solution 2:

        • _____

        • _____

        • _____

One Solution, Multiple Reasons

▷ Body Paragraph 1: Summary of an Article

   ▷ Topic Sentence: (includes name of the author, title of the article, and main idea of

   the article) _____

     _____

      ▷ Important Information from the Article:

        • _____

        • _____

        • _____

▶ Body Paragraph 2: Reason 1 to Support the Proposed Solution

   ▶ Topic Sentence: _____

      _____

      ▶ Supporting Reasons and Evidence for Reason 1:

         • _____

         • _____

         • _____

▶ Body Paragraph 3: Reason 2 to Support the Proposed Solution

   ▶ Topic Sentence: _____

      _____

      ▶ Supporting Reasons and Evidence for Reason 2:

         • _____

         • _____

         • _____

B. Checking in. *Share your outline with a partner. Did your partner . . .*

- provide enough information about the problem in the summary paragraph?
- propose one or more reasonable solutions?
- support the solution(s) with enough reasons and evidence?

Based on your partner's feedback, you may want to rewrite parts of your outline.

■ THE CONCLUSION

In the conclusion to a problem-solution essay, clearly restate the problem and the proposed solution(s). You can end with a call to action, either to the general audience of readers or the specific people who have the power to implement your solution. Or you can use one of the other concluding strategies from previous units, such as

- placing the issue in a larger context
- presenting an alternate point of view
- looking to the future

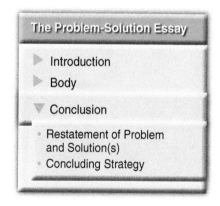

The Problem-Solution Essay

▶ Introduction
▶ Body
▼ Conclusion
   • Restatement of Problem and Solution(s)
   • Concluding Strategy

Focused Practice

Read the model of a concluding paragraph and complete the tasks.

> In brief, the continued use of performance-enhancing drugs will lead to more suspicion and disappointment for athletes and fans. However, if young people and adult athletes are well informed about the dangers of drugs and the value of good sportsmanship, the problems with drugs will diminish. As fans of the Olympics, the Tour de France, and other exciting sporting events, we need to support athletes who don't take drugs. As parents, coaches, and teachers, we need to help create a healthy athletic culture.

1. Circle the transition words that introduce the conclusion.
2. Underline the sentence that restates the problem.
3. Double underline the sentence that restates the solution.
4. Check (✓) the sentences that call for action. Who is asked to perform the action?

Your Own Writing

Planning Your Conclusion

A. *What will you put in your conclusion? List your ideas here.*

_____

_____

B. *How will you restate the problem and solution?*

   1. Write the sentence that will restate the problem.

_____

_____

   2. Write the sentence that will restate the solution.

_____

_____

C. *What strategy will you use to close the essay?*

_____

_____

D. **Checking in.** *Share your ideas with a partner. Did your partner . . .*

- choose an effective strategy?
- restate the problem and solution in a new and interesting way?

Writing Your First Draft

A. *Read the* **Tip for Writers.** *Review your notes on pages 133, 137, and 145–147. Then write the first draft of your essay. When you are finished, give your essay a working title.*

> **Tip for Writers**
>
> When you write your first draft, be sure that you provide enough evidence to convince the reader that the problem exists and is serious.

B. *After you write the first draft, put in citations for any sources of information that you used. Use MLA (Modern Language Association) style for citations within and at the end of your essay. See Unit 2 (pages 49–50) and the Appendix on pages 194–195 for more information on MLA style.*

C. *Hand in your draft to your teacher.*

Revising your work is an essential part of the writing process. This is your opportunity to be sure that your essay has all the important pieces and that it is clear.

Focused Practice

A. *You have read parts of this problem-solution essay. Now read the entire essay to see how the parts fit together.*

Ending the Drug Problem in Sports

International sporting events provide an opportunity for athletes from around the world to compete in a healthy environment, away from the usual stress of international relations. Events such as the Olympics and the Commonwealth games are popular because the citizens of each country can cheer for their teams in fair contests. However, not all athletes follow the rules; some of them secretly take drugs. These drugs have ruined the careers of several talented athletes, who have disappointed their fans and fellow citizens. Performance-enhancing drugs can unfairly advantage some athletes and seriously damage their health, so young people and adult athletes need to be educated about the dangers of these substances.

According to Vrinda Maheshwari in "Athletes and drugs: an abusive relationship," the use of performance-enhancing drugs in international sporting events has become a big problem for which there is no clear solution. The drug allegations at the 2010 Commonwealth Games have led Maheshwari to wonder if the athletes will ever stop using drugs. A spokesperson for the Commonwealth Games said that regular drug-testing by the National Anti-Doping Agency has not ended the problem. Athletes have always tried to boost their performance, and modern drugs have created an atmosphere of suspicion in sports. The most common performance-boosting drugs are human-growth hormones, anabolic steroids, beta-blockers, erythropoietin, stimulants, and diuretics. In addition to providing an unfair advantage to those who use them, these drugs also can damage the health of the athletes and have even caused death. Although some agencies are printing lists of banned substances and athletes suffer severe penalties when caught, so far no solutions to this problem have proved effective.

The best way to approach this difficult problem is to educate young people about the dangers of performance-enhancing drugs. The competitive atmosphere of athletic training can put pressure on athletes who begin training at a young age. Therefore, coaches and training camps for these young athletes need to tell them about the unfairness of cheating and the dangers to health. Not only young athletes in training, but also other children and teenagers need to be educated because they can be easily influenced by peer groups who accept the use of drugs. In some popular sports, performance-enhancing drugs have become part of the culture. For example, in the sport of bodybuilding, anabolic steroids, which can damage the liver and reproductive systems, are common. Young people can find a lot of misinformation about the drugs on the Internet, and may even see real or fake drugs for sale. Although it is important for schools, parents, teams, and media to present accurate information about the dangers of these substances, it is even more important for them to teach all children that cheating and unfair advantages have no place in good sportsmanship.

However, the education campaign can't end with young people because adult athletes need specific information about the drugs, their side effects, and possible penalties. They need to know that penalties can be serious. Maheshwari points out, for example, that the Canadian track star Ben Johnson lost his Olympic medals when he was disqualified for taking drugs. Moreover, since the penalties alone haven't solved the problem, the sporting events need to do more. The International Association of Athletics Federations has made a good start by publishing a list of illegal substances. It's possible that the list could change as new drugs are developed, so it needs to be updated every year. Because researchers are discovering new side effects of existing drugs, athletes need to remain informed in order to protect themselves. If the rules are clear and consistent and the penalties strictly enforced, athletes will be more likely to follow the rules. Athletes who want to attract fans should find fair and legal ways to prepare for competitions.

In brief, the continued use of performance-enhancing drugs will lead to more suspicion and disappointment for athletes and fans. However, if young people and adult athletes are well informed about the dangers of drugs and the value of good sportsmanship, the problems with drugs will diminish. As fans of the Olympics,

(continued)

the Tour de France, and other exciting sporting events, we need to support athletes who don't take drugs. As parents, coaches, and teachers, we need to help create a healthy athletic culture.

Work Cited

Maheshwari, Vrinda. "Athletes and drugs: an abusive relationship."
thedailymaverick.com. The Daily Maverick (South Africa), 14 Oct. 2010. Web.
27 Feb. 2011.

B. *Work with a partner. Answer the questions about the essay on pages 150–152.*

1. What is the thesis statement? Underline it.

2. Which paragraph summarizes an article about the problem? _____
   Underline the author, title, and main idea of the article.

3. What solution is proposed in paragraph 3? Underline the sentence that states it.

4. What solution is proposed in paragraph 4? Underline the sentence that states it.

5. What words connect the parts of the essay? Circle them.

6. Find reasons and evidence to support each solution. Check (✓) each reason you find.
   Put an X next to each example.

C. Checking in. *Discuss your marked-up essays with another pair of students. Then in your group, share which part of the essay you found most convincing. Do you agree with the proposed solutions? Why or why not?*

Building Word Knowledge

The writer included verb + preposition and adjective + preposition combinations in "Ending the Drug Problem in Sports." Write your own sentences using each of the following verb + preposition or adjective + preposition combinations.

1. The citizens of each country can **cheer for** their teams.

   _____

   _____

2. Ben Johnson lost his Olympic medals when he **was disqualified for** taking drugs.

   _____

   _____

3. The continued use of performance-enhancing drugs will **lead to** more suspicion and disappointment for athletes and fans.

_____

_____

4. Athletes who want to attract fans should find fair and legal ways to **prepare for** competitions.

_____

_____

Your Own Writing

Revising Your Draft

A. *Reread the first draft of your essay. Use the Revision Checklist to identify parts of your writing that might need improvement.*

B. *Review your plans and notes, and your responses to the Revision Checklist. Then revise your first draft. Save your revised essay. You will look at it again in the next section.*

Revision Checklist

Did you . . .

☐ state the problem and proposed solution(s) in your thesis statement?

☐ provide enough background information in your introduction?

☐ summarize an article about a problem in sports in your first body paragraph?

☐ propose one or more solutions to the problem in your remaining body paragraphs?

☐ provide enough reasons and evidence to support your solution(s)?

☐ connect the parts of your essay with effective transition words and strategies?

☐ restate the problem and solution(s) in your conclusion?

☐ use an effective concluding strategy?

☐ use correct verb + preposition and adjective + preposition combinations?

☐ give your essay a good title?

☐ cite sources you used in your essay?

■ GRAMMAR PRESENTATION

Before you hand in your revised essay, you must check it for any errors in grammar, punctuation, and spelling. In this section, you will learn about adverb clauses. You will focus on this grammar when you edit and proofread your essay.

Adverb Clauses

Grammar Notes	Examples
1. A **clause** is a group of words that contains at least one subject and a verb showing past, present, or future time. Clauses are either independent or dependent.	• **Sports fans all over the world watch the games on TV** when the Olympics are on.
Independent clauses (also called main clauses) can stand alone as complete sentences.	_independent clause_ _dependent clause_ • **The athlete was nervous** when the race began.
Dependent clauses (also called subordinate clauses) cannot stand alone. They need another clause to be fully understood. **Note:** The clauses can come in either order. If the dependent clause comes first, we place a comma after it.	_dependent clause_ _independent clause_ • **Before the games begin,** athletes are tested for drugs.
2. **Adverb clauses** are dependent clauses that indicate **how, when, where, why,** or **under what conditions** things happen. Adverb clauses may also introduce a contrast.	• Athletes can't compete in the Olympics **unless they train for a long time.** _(condition)_ • **Even though athletes are tested,** drugs continue to be a problem. _(contrast)_
Adverb clauses begin with **subordinating conjunctions** (also called subordinating adverbs), which can be either single words or phrases.	• He avoids steroid use **now that he understands the dangers.**
3. **Adverb clauses of time** indicate **when** something happens. They are introduced by _after, as, as soon as, before, by the time, once, since, until / till, when, whenever, while,_ etc.	• Ben Johnson lost his Olympic medals **when he was disqualified for taking drugs.**
Be Careful! Use present tense verbs in adverb clauses of future events.	• **When young people are educated about the dangers,** drug use will diminish. Not: When young people ~~will be~~ educated about the dangers, drug use will diminish.

4. **Adverb clauses of place** indicate **where** something happens. They are introduced by *anywhere, everywhere, where, wherever,* etc.

- **Wherever you travel during the Olympics,** you find sports fans watching the games.

5. **Adverb clauses of reason** indicate **why** something happens. They are introduced by *as, because, now that* (= because now), *since,* etc.

- It's difficult to tell if all the athletes are following the rules **because some of them are secretly taking drugs that enhance their performance**.

6. **Adverb clauses of condition** indicate **under what conditions** something happens. They are introduced by *even if, if, only if, unless, in case,* etc.

- **If young people and adult athletes are well informed of the dangers of drugs and the value of good sportsmanship,** the problems with drugs will diminish.

7. **Adverb clauses of contrast** make a contrast with the idea expressed in the independent clause. They are introduced by *although, even though, though, whereas, while,* etc.

- **Although some agencies are printing lists of banned substances and athletes suffer severe penalties when caught,** so far no solutions to this problem have proved effective.

Focused Practice

A. *The Tour de France is a bicycle race that takes place every summer in France. Use subordinating conjunctions to combine these sentences about the race. The first sentence is combined for you.*

1. The race begins. All the hotels along the route are filled with spectators. (*time*)

    When the race begins, all the hotels along the route are filled with spectators.

2. The cyclists ride along the long route. They are followed by a caravan of floats tossing candy to children. (*place*)

    _____

    _____

3. The 2010 winner was suspended from the sport. He had a positive drug test. (*reason*)

    _____

    _____

4. You want to see the entire race. You need to watch it on television. (*condition*)

    _____

    _____

5. Doping scandals have become common. The race goes on every year. (*contrast*)

    _____

    _____

B. *Look at the timeline of the life of Lance Armstrong. Then write sentences about his life using adverb clauses. The first sentence is written for you.*

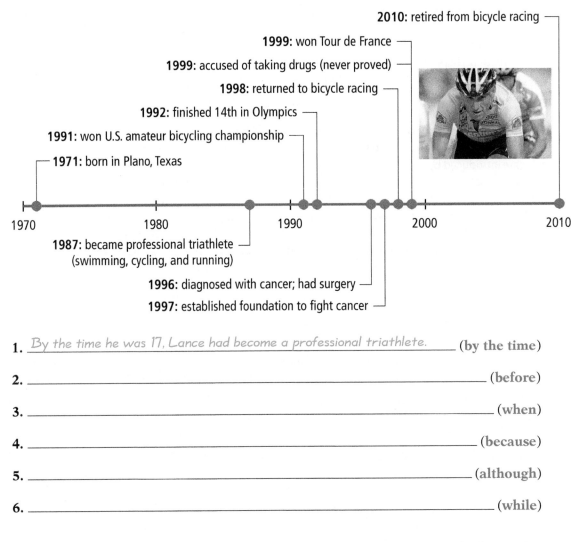

2010: retired from bicycle racing

1999: won Tour de France

1999: accused of taking drugs (never proved)

1998: returned to bicycle racing

1992: finished 14th in Olympics

1991: won U.S. amateur bicycling championship

1971: born in Plano, Texas

1970   1980   1990   2000   2010

1987: became professional triathlete
(swimming, cycling, and running)

1996: diagnosed with cancer; had surgery

1997: established foundation to fight cancer

1. *By the time he was 17, Lance had become a professional triathlete.* **(by the time)**

2. _____ **(before)**

3. _____ **(when)**

4. _____ **(because)**

5. _____ **(although)**

6. _____ **(while)**

C. *Read and edit the paragraph. There are six mistakes in the use of adverb clauses. The first one is corrected for you. Correct the other five.*

> *because*
> Performance-enhancing drugs should be legal for adult athletes ~~although~~ they are old enough to make their own decisions. Adults can read the research on side effects and consult with doctors. Just as they do for other drugs. In any case, drugs don't advantage the users any more than other uses of technology in modern sports, such as high-tech training machines, shoes, and clothing. For example, when Michael Phelps competed in the 2008 Olympics his swimsuit cost $550. Fans say they are disappointed in athletes who break the rules, but sports have always been about winning, and athletes do whatever will help them win. Even the drugs hurt their bodies, it's possible the sports themselves will injure them more. Well-

paid athletes continue to play sports. Because the rewards make it all worthwhile. If we will continue to punish athletes for taking performance-enhancing drugs, we will waste time and lose many great athletes.

D. *Write five sentences related to the assignment you chose on page 132. Use adverb clauses. These may be sentences you already have in your essay.*

1. _____

_____

2. _____

_____

3. _____

_____

4. _____

_____

5. _____

_____

Your Own Writing

Editing Your Draft

A. *Use the Editing Checklist to edit and proofread your essay.*

B. *Prepare a clean copy of the final draft of your essay and hand it in to your teacher.*

Editing Checklist
Did you . . .
☐ include adverb clauses and use them correctly?
☐ use correct verb forms, punctuation, and spelling?
☐ use verb + preposition and adjective + preposition combinations and other words correctly?

UNIT 6 Communities

IN THIS UNIT You will be writing an essay about the communities in which people choose to live. In your essay, you will use more than one organizational structure.

Many retired people are now choosing to live in active retirement communities with other seniors as their neighbors. Most of these communities have a few thousand residents, but some are as large as small cities. Most of the residents are active enough to enjoy the many opportunities for classes, recreation, and other social activities. Young people are allowed to visit, but no one under a certain age, often 55, is allowed to buy property or live there. Do you believe that an active retirement community is a good option for older people?

Planning for Writing

◼ BRAINSTORM

A. *For this activity, your teacher will divide the class into three equal groups and assign one activity to each group. Group members can work together or in pairs.*

1. Using a T-chart. *On a separate piece of paper, make a T-chart listing the advantages (e.g., opportunities for recreation) and disadvantages (e.g., distance from family) of living in an active retirement community.*

2. Using a Venn Diagram. *On a separate piece of paper, use a Venn diagram to list similarities and differences between active retirement communities (with people age 55 and older) and conventional communities (with people of all ages).*

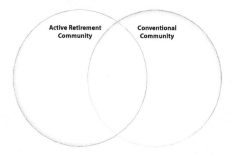

3. Using a Brainstorming Map. *On a separate piece of paper, create a brainstorming map to explore the effects of an age-restricted active retirement community (e.g., effects on residents, families, and societies).*

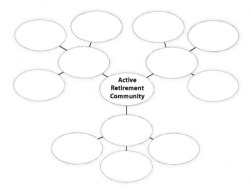

B. *Students from each group will present their findings to the class. Take notes during the presentations and discuss the following questions with a partner.*

1. What were the most important advantages and disadvantages that you learned from Group 1?

2. What were the most interesting similarities and differences that you learned from Group 2?

3. What were the most significant effects that you learned from Group 3?

■ **READ**

Read the magazine article on active retirement communities.

TIME

Not Your Mother's Retirement Community

1   If there's one thing older folks are said to dread,[1] it's the prospect of a retirement community—that residential departure lounge[2] from this life to whatever comes next. Filled with infirm[3] neighbors and too-little stimulation, they are widely seen as one step above a nursing home[4]—if only because you maintain your own little home—but not much more. That, at least, is the way they used to be.

2   As with so much else in the baby boomers'[5] long march from birth to senescence,[6] retirement communities are being reinvented— and with good reason. Only a generation or two ago, simple actuarial[7] arithmetic didn't give most retirees a whole lot of years to fill after they quit work. Those with the means[8] would fly south or west for a few quiet years of shuffleboard or bingo at places like Del Webb's famed Sun City developments in Arizona before passing into dependent old age. But the health and wealth that many boomers are bringing into retirement are giving them 25 years or more to play with, not to mention the resources to spend that time well. For them, an early dinner and an evening of board games is not going to be enough.

3   To attract today's more youthful retirees, who may be working part time or even full time at a hobby business, developers are rethinking all aspects of the classic adult-retirement village. They are building what they call active-adult communities for folks as young as 55 in places like Colorado, Michigan, and New Jersey to accommodate those who want to stay immersed in the world, even as

they step back from some of its daily nuisances.[9] The new developments ensure mobility, with access to mass transit and garages for residents who own their own cars, which make visits to family members or commutes into town easy. They are also offering a stunning mix of activities, including such options as kayaking and skydiving. They include spa-level fitness and wellness centers, college-level academic courses, resort-level concierge[10] services, and gourmet dining.

4   Such changes are the fruits of both good planning and good business sense. Developers have had six decades to anticipate the boomers' retirement, and they have long been plotting ways to woo them. Lately, they've been putting their plans into action. "The senior-housing business has changed dramatically over the last seven or eight

---

[1] **dread:** fear
[2] **lounge:** a public room in a hotel, airport, or other building where people can relax, sit down, or drink
[3] **infirm:** weak or sick, especially because of age
[4] **nursing home:** a place where people who are too old or too sick to take care of themselves can live
[5] **baby boomers:** people born between 1946 and 1964
[6] **senescence:** old age
[7] **actuarial:** calculations of risk, especially in the insurance industry
[8] **means:** money or income a person has
[9] **nuisances:** things that annoy or cause you problems
[10] **concierge:** an employee who helps residents with things such as home maintenance, meal reservations, and travel arrangements

160   UNIT 6

years," says David Schless, president of the American Senior Housing Association. Nearly half of retirement-community managers intend to at least upgrade their fitness centers this year or next, and a similar percentage said they had already done so in the previous two years, according to a survey by the International Council on Active Aging.

5   Not all active-adult communities are the same, of course, and in many cases, their location determines what they offer. Trilogy at the Vineyards, near San Francisco, for example, has a wine-country feel to attract locals who don't want to give up the Napa Valley wine region lifestyle and émigrés[11] who want to adopt it. Anthem Ranch, near Denver, takes advantage of its ski-country site, making it easy for residents to hit the slopes[12] or hike the mountains.

6   St. Joe Co., which develops retirement communities and other residences, is building on thousands of acres in northwest Florida and stresses the connectivity of its homes—and not just high-speed Internet but also proximity to transportation, including an airport. Both are essential for people who continue to work, and for a new breed of retiree that Jerry Ray, senior vice president of St. Joe, calls "splitters"—people with two full-time residences, one in the South and one elsewhere. St. Joe even donated 4,000 acres (1,600 hectares) to a new international airport near Panama City, Fla., which will serve both locals and retirees expected to move to the area.

7   If you think an active-adult community might be for you:

• EXAMINE THE FEATURES. Does the community offer enough of the activities you enjoy? How popular are the programs? It'll be a lonely scuba trip if you're the only one who signs up.

• THINK AHEAD. Some day you'll value a first-floor bedroom, large handles on cabinets, and being near a hospital. Also, if you work, the fitness-center hours and other activities may not suit your schedule.

• VISIT MORE THAN ONCE. Don't take a sales agent's word for it; visit residents and ask about the things that matter to you. While you're at it, take note of their age. The last thing you want is to end up being the lone kid (or geezer)[13] on the block.

---

[11] **émigrés:** people who leave their own country (or region) to live in another
[12] **hit the slopes:** to ski
[13] **geezer:** slang term for an elderly person

Building Word Knowledge

Understanding and Using Figurative Language. Writers often use words and phrases in ways that differ from their ordinary meaning. Sometimes they compare their subjects to something entirely different to make a point. In the following example from "Not Your Mother's Retirement Community," the writer compares a retirement community to a departure lounge (waiting room) in an airport:

Example:

If there's one thing older folks are said to dread, it's the prospect of a retirement community—that residential departure lounge from this life to whatever comes next.

This comparison implies that older folks view retirement communities as a place to wait for whatever comes after the end of life.

Look at the highlighted examples of figurative language from "Not Your Mother's Retirement Community." Match each example with its meaning. The first one is done for you.

__b__ **1.** . . . the baby boomers' **long march** from birth to senescence . . .

_____ **2.** . . . active-adult communities for folks as young as 55 in places like Colorado, Michigan and New Jersey to accommodate those who want to **stay immersed in the world**, . . .

_____ **3.** . . . even as they **step back from** some of its daily nuisances.

_____ **4.** Such changes are **the fruits** of both good planning and good business sense.

_____ **5.** Developers have had six decades to anticipate the boomers' retirement, and they have long been plotting **ways to woo them**.

_____ **6.** The last thing you want is to end up being **the lone kid (or geezer) on the block**.

a. the good results

b. journey of many years

c. methods to attract them

d. remove themselves from

e. the only person there

f. remain active in society

Focused Practice

A. *Read the* Tip for Writers. *Work with a partner. Discuss the writer's tone in the article "Not Your Mother's Retirement Community."*

B. *Look at the pairs of words below. Circle the word from each pair that best describes the author's overall tone in the article. Then find an example from the text to illustrate your choice. (Keep in mind that an essay or article would not typically have two contrasting tones, such as* serious *and* playful.*) The first one is done for you.*

1. serious (playful) "older folks are said to dread"

   (rhyming words: said, dread)

2. formal   informal   _____

3. negative positive   _____

4. distant   friendly   _____

C. *Work with a partner. Find each phrase in the article and decide whether it describes the old-style (old) or new-style (new) retirement community. The first one is done for you.*

old **1.** that residential departure lounge from this life to whatever comes next

_____ **2.** access to mass transit

_____ **3.** garages for residents who own their own cars

_____ **4.** one step above a nursing home

_____ **5.** high-speed Internet

_____ **6.** a few quiet years of shuffleboard or bingo

_____ **7.** a stunning mix of activities

_____ **8.** gourmet dining

D. The article "Not Your Mother's Retirement Community" presents one possible living arrangement for retired people, but there are others. Think about retired people in your native country or culture. Where do they live? What kinds of activities do they enjoy?

Write a paragraph describing the typical living arrangements for retired people in your native country or culture. Select your words carefully so that your paragraph has a reasonable tone.

To maintain a reasonable tone . . .

- *do not* use overly judgmental words such as *ridiculous or stupid* to describe the topic.

- *do not* offer excessive praise or overgeneralizations, such as *the best in the world* or *the only right way*.

_____

_____

_____

_____

_____

_____

_____

_____

_____

_____

Writing an Essay with Two or More Structures

You are going to write an essay about the communities or households in which people choose to live. When you write an essay on a complex topic, you may need to examine it in different ways. For example, in essays where you present an opinion on a controversial topic or suggest a solution to a problem, you might decide to analyze causes or effects and make a comparison. In the essay in this unit, you will include paragraphs using at least two organizational structures.

The Essay
▶ Introduction
▶ Body
▶ Conclusion

Like all essays, your essay here will have three parts.

Step 1   Prewriting

For an essay using multiple organizational structures, the prewriting step involves exploring and selecting the organizational structures that will best support your thesis. For example, if you are writing an essay in favor of one living situation, it may be important to both discuss its advantages and compare it to an alternative living situation. The prewriting step also includes brainstorming ideas to add specific support for your points.

Your Own Writing

Choosing Your Assignment

A. *Choose Assignment 1 or Assignment 2.*

1. Many families with small children live in cities in order to be close to employment and cultural opportunities. Others live in suburban areas in order to enjoy the child-centered lifestyle and safe streets. Still others choose to live in the countryside, where they can raise their children working on the land. In your opinion, which place is the best for raising children? Why is it the best place?

   To support your point of view, you may discuss the place's advantages and disadvantages and its effects on the residents. If you wish, compare the best place with the alternatives.

2. In some families, several generations live in the same house or apartment. These include grandparents, parents, and children, and sometimes uncles, aunts, and cousins. Do you believe that a multi-generational household is a good living arrangement for everyone involved? Why?

   To support your point of view, you may discuss the advantages and disadvantages of this type of living arrangement, as well as its effects on the various residents. If you wish, compare this living situation to the alternative: households in which grandparents live apart from their children and grandchildren.

B. *Freewrite for 10 minutes on your assignment. Here are some questions to get you started:*

- What do you already know about the living situations?

- Have you lived in or visited an urban, suburban, or rural area (Assignment 1) or a multi-generational home (Assignment 2)?

- Why are these topics interesting to you?

- What more do you want to find out about them?

C. **Checking in.** *Work with a partner who chose the same assignment. Discuss the ideas and details you wrote in Exercise B. Did your partner . . .*

- describe a particular living situation?

- express an opinion about the living situation?

- explain why he or she finds the living situation interesting?

Share your point of view on your partner's topic. Based on your discussion make changes and additions to your writing.

D. *Complete the three prewriting activities below on a separate piece of paper. Fill in as much information as you can. Keep these graphic organizers. You will have a chance to review, change, or add information to them later in the unit.*

1. Make a T-chart like the one on page 159 to list advantages and disadvantages of a living situation.

   - If you chose Assignment 1, list advantages and disadvantages of the community you chose to write about as the best place for raising children.

   - If you chose Assignment 2, list advantages and disadvantages of a multi-generational household.

2. Make a Venn diagram like the one on page 159 to list similarities and differences between two living situations.

   - If you chose Assignment 1, list similarities and differences between life in the community that you chose to write about and life in another kind of community.

   - If you chose Assignment 2, list similarities and differences between life in a multi-generational household and life in a parent-child only household.

3. Create a brainstorming map like the one on page 159 to explore the effects of an urban, suburban, or rural community or of a multi-generational household.

■THE INTRODUCTION

You have practiced three opening strategies for essays, using

- an interesting or surprising fact.
- a thoughtful question.
- an interesting example.

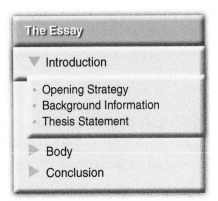

Another effective strategy is to begin with a relevant *quotation*. Use a quotation from someone connected to the topic of your essay, *not* a well-known quotation from a famous person, which may already be overly familiar to your readers.

In an essay using multiple organizational structures, you will open with one of these strategies. Your thesis statement will express your opinion on the question in the assignment.

Example:

Essay Assignment: Many retired people are choosing to live in active retirement communities. Do you believe that an active retirement community is a good choice for retired people?

In supporting your point of view, you may discuss the advantages and disadvantages of these communities and their effects on the residents. If you wish, compare retirement communities with other options for the elderly.

Thesis Statement: Active retirement communities are a good choice for retired people because they offer important advantages over other options.

Remember: A successful thesis statement . . .

- presents the controlling idea of the entire essay.
- responds to the assignment.
- contains an idea the writer will develop and support.
- does more than state a fact. It usually presents an arguable assertion or claim.

You have also learned that the introductory paragraph in an essay gives background information to help the reader understand the thesis statement. (To review the elements of an introductory paragraph, look back at Unit 1, pages 8–9.)

Focused Practice

A. *Reread the essay assignment in the example above. Then decide which information you might use as background information for an introductory paragraph on the topic. Check (✓) the sentences you choose and discuss your choices with a partner.*

- Ask yourself this question to help you: *Is this information important?*
- Give reasons for your choices when you and your partner have different opinions.

_____ **1.** the number of active retirement communities in the world

_____ **2.** a description of the largest active retirement community

_____ **3.** some of the services offered at retirement communities

_____ **4.** the age rules of the communities

_____ **5.** a few important criticisms of the effects of age-restricted communities

_____ **6.** the yearly cost of an active retirement community

_____ **7.** a comparison of retirement communities and nursing homes

B. *Read the introduction for the essay assignment on page 166. Then with a partner, complete the chart with words from the introduction.*

> Mary Alice Stephen loves living in Oakmont Village in Santa Rosa, California. "We have 87 interest groups, in everything from politics to yoga," she says. "And if that's not enough for you, you can start another one." Like millions of other seniors around the world, Mary Alice hopes to enjoy many years of active retirement in a community that doesn't allow anyone under the age of 55 to buy or even rent property. These active retirement communities, which offer small individual homes or apartments, recreational facilities, and services for seniors, have been criticized for removing seniors from the real world where they have spent their lives. Even worse, that real world includes the children and grandchildren with whom they could be spending their last years. However, even with these drawbacks, active retirement communities are a good choice for retired people because they offer important advantages over other options.

Relevant Quotation

Background Information from Exercise A

1.

2.

3.

Writer's Point of View (Thesis Statement)

C. *Reread the thesis statement on page 166. With a partner, discuss what makes it a good thesis statement.*

D. *Complete the checklist for the other possible thesis statements for the essay assignment on page 166. Check (✓) the items that are true for each statement.*

1. **Thesis Statement:** I would never send my parents to live in any kind of retirement community.

_____ **a.** Presents the controlling idea of the entire essay *(Could an entire essay be written on this?)*

_____ **b.** Responds to the assignment

_____ **c.** Contains an idea that the writer will develop and support

_____ **d.** Does more than state a fact—usually presents an arguable assertion or claim

2. **Thesis Statement:** I believe that active retirement communities are not a good option because they remove seniors from their families and communities.

_____ **a.** Presents the controlling idea of the entire essay *(Could an entire essay be written on this?)*

_____ **b.** Responds to the assignment

_____ **c.** Contains an idea that the writer will develop and support

_____ **d.** Does more than state a fact—usually presents an arguable assertion or claim

3. **Thesis Statement:** The benefits of active retirement communities far outweigh the drawbacks.

_____ **a.** Presents the controlling idea of the entire essay *(Could an entire essay be written on this?)*

_____ **b.** Responds to the assignment

_____ **c.** Contains an idea that the writer will develop and support

_____ **d.** Does more than state a fact—usually presents an arguable assertion or claim

4. **Thesis Statement:** Active retirement communities are becoming popular in many countries.

_____ **a.** Presents the controlling idea of the entire essay *(Could an entire essay be written on this?)*

_____ **b.** Responds to the assignment

_____ **c.** Contains an idea that the writer will develop and support

_____ **d.** Does more than state a fact—usually presents an arguable assertion or claim

Your Own Writing

Finding Out More

A. *Learn more about the topic you chose for your essay. Research the topic online or at the library.*

- If you chose Assignment 1, find out more about life in the kind of community you want to write about. You may want to use the following keywords when you search for information online: *urban/suburban/rural schools, crime, communities, recreation.*

  You may also want to survey your friends, relatives, and classmates who have children. Ask them about life in an urban / suburban / rural community. Possible survey questions:

  - What are the benefits for children of living in an urban/suburban/rural community?

  - What are the drawbacks?

  - Why did you choose (or remain in) this living situation?

  - What special problems are there for parents?

- If you chose Assignment 2, find out more about life in a multi-generational household. You may want to use the following keywords when you search for information online: *multi-generational household, extended family*

  You may also want to survey your friends, relatives, and classmates who have lived in multi-generational households. Possible survey questions:

  - What are the benefits of living in a multi-generational household?

  - What are the drawbacks?

  - Why did your family choose this living situation?

  - What special problems are there for you as a grandparent/parent/son/daughter/ cousin?

  Interview members from various age groups to get a variety of perspectives. Keep track of your survey results and use the numbers in your essay. Record interesting quotations on the subject of multi-generational living situations. When you use a quotation in your essay, be sure to spell the speaker's name correctly.

B. *Take notes on what you found out. For example:*

- Record key information about the community you want to write about.

- Note the sources for your information.

- If you are using quotations, record the speakers' exact words, the names of the people you interviewed, and the dates of the interviews.

- Add relevant information to the T-chart, Venn diagram, and brainstorming map you created earlier in the unit.

Use this information when you write your essay.

C. Checking In. *Share your information with a partner. Did your partner . . .*

- gather enough facts and details about a living situation?

- add any relevant personal observations and experience?

Planning Your Introduction

A. *Find an interesting quotation to open your introduction and catch your reader's attention. Write it below.*

_____

_____

B. *List the background information you will need to include in your introduction.*

_____

_____

_____

C. *Write a draft of your thesis statement. Make sure your thesis statement answers the question in the assignment and clearly presents your point of view. Look back at your freewriting, T-chart, Venn diagram, and brainstorming map to help you.*

_____

_____

D. Checking in. *Share your thesis statement with a partner. Does your partner's thesis statement . . .*

- present the controlling idea of the entire essay?

- respond to the assignment?

- contain an idea that your partner will develop and support?

- do more than state a fact?

Tell your partner what kind of supporting evidence you expect to see in his or her essay, based on the thesis statement. Based on your partner's feedback, you may want to rewrite your thesis statement.

■ THE BODY

In this unit, the overall purpose of your essay will be to persuade the reader of your point of view. In exploring your subject and supporting your point of view, you will select at least two organizational structures.

In previous units, you wrote essays that were organized according to the following structures:

- persuasion

- comparison and contrast

- cause-effect analysis

- problem-solution

In an essay using multiple organizational structures, you will select the structures that will most effectively support your thesis statement for the body paragraphs of your essay.

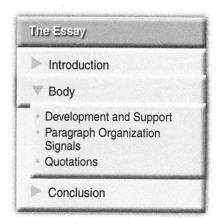

The Essay

▶ Introduction

▼ Body
  · Development and Support
  · Paragraph Organization Signals
  · Quotations

▶ Conclusion

Developing and Supporting Your Thesis Statement

Look at the possible organizational structures that can be used to develop the following thesis statement. To help decide which structures to use in your body paragraphs, ask yourself questions such as the ones listed below. The answers may also help you write topic sentences and organize your body paragraphs.

Example:

Thesis Statement: In spite of several drawbacks, active retirement communities are a good choice for retired people because they offer important advantages over other options.

Persuasion

Ask yourself: What are the advantages of the communities?
                 What is the opposing point of view?

Comparison and Contrast

Ask yourself: What are the other most common options for retired people?
                 What are the differences and/or similarities between the options?

Cause-Effect Analysis

Ask yourself: What are the effects of the retirement communities on residents?
                 What are the effects on their families?
                 What are the effects on society?

Problem and Proposed Solution(s)

Ask yourself: What problem do people face when they retire from work and grow older?
                 What solution(s) do I support?

Focused Practice

A. *For the following thesis statement, write questions using each of the strategies. The first one is done for you.*

Thesis Statement: I believe that active retirement communities are not a good option because they remove seniors from their families and communities.

1. Persuasion

Ask yourself: <u>Why should seniors remain in their families and communities?</u>

<u>What is the opposing point of view?</u>

2. Comparison and Contrast

Ask yourself: _____

_____

3. Cause-Effect Analysis

Ask yourself: _____

_____

4. Problem-Solution

Ask yourself: _____

_____

B. *Read the following example. Then choose one of the organizational structures from Exercise A. Copy and answer the questions you wrote and write a topic sentence for a body paragraph.*

Example:

Organizational Structure: Persuasion

Ask yourself:	Why should seniors remain in their families and communities?
Possible answer:	Seniors should remain in their families and communities because they still have a lot to contribute to them. For example, they can help raise grandchildren and do volunteer work.
Ask yourself:	What is the opposing point of view?
Possible answer:	Seniors can become a burden to their families and communities. They begin to need extra care and services.
Possible topic sentence:	Although they can eventually become a burden, most seniors still have a lot to offer to their families and communities during their retirement years.

Organizational Structure: _____

Ask yourself: _____

_____

Possible answer: _____

_____

Ask yourself: _____

_____

Possible answer: _____

_____

Possible topic sentence: _____

_____

Signaling Paragraph Organization

When using multiple organizational structures, writers often use words and phrases that tell the reader which organizational structure is being used in the paragraph. This helps the reader follow the writer's reasoning and see how the paragraph supports the thesis statement.

The following body paragraph uses a compare-contrast organizational structure to support the thesis statement. The sentence that signals the organization is underlined. Note that in order to explain why many people choose to live in active retirement communities, the writer compares and contrasts these subjects:

- life in the towns and cities where people have spent their whole lives
- life in active retirement communities

Example:

Thesis Statement: In spite of several drawbacks, active retirement communities are a good choice for retired people because they offer important advantages over other options.

When people reach the end of their work lives and are no longer geographically tied to their jobs, they have the option of untying all their other knots and moving to a new community that appeals to them more. When comparing their current neighborhoods with active retirement communities, people consider many factors. It is true that the towns and cities where they have lived their whole lives have much to offer, including a diversity of age groups and their activities. Retired people enjoy having the time to volunteer in neighborhood schools, stroll in interesting shopping districts, and see their familiar neighbors.

(continued)

However, although many retired people would regret leaving these opportunities, they wouldn't miss many of the negative sides of their age-diverse neighborhoods. Children can be noisy, and cities can be dangerous. Most retirement communities are safe, quiet havens far from crime and pollution. Some are even far from the cold weather that many older people detest. In Europe, for example, most retirement communities are opening in warm regions, such as southern Spain, where retirees from the cold north flock like birds who have flown south for their last winters.

The following list includes words and phrases that can signal the different organizational structures of a body paragraph to a reader.

Persuasion

- *advantage / disadvantage*
- *benefit / drawback*
- *agree / disagree*
- *although, even though, while, whereas* (signal an opposing point of view)
- *We cannot deny that . . .* (expresses acknowledgment)

Comparison and Contrast

- *compare / contrast, in comparison, in contrast*
- *like / unlike*
- *similarly, in the same way, just as*
- *on the other hand, however*
- *on the contrary, conversely*

Cause-Effect Analysis

- *cause, result in, affect, lead to*
- *because, since*
- *therefore, consequently, thus*
- *as a result of, because of*

Problem-Solution

- *problem, issue, dilemma*
- *solve, solution*

Focused Practice

Read the following body paragraphs. Underline the sentence that signals the organizational structure and circle the specific clue words and phrases. Then write the organizational structure below.

1.

The move from north to south, or city to suburban or rural area, can separate seniors from their children and grandchildren, depriving them of the chance to see their grandchildren on a regular basis. While their families might object to this, the seniors themselves enjoy the advantage of increased independence. Until recent years, the tradition in Spain has been for retirees to live with their grown children, but 77-year-old Spaniard Fernando Feliz is certain that he doesn't want to live with his. "I don't want to be a burden to anybody . . . I know what it was like when my wife took care of her mother, and I don't want that for my children" (Fuchs). Retirement communities are designed to support the independence of the residents. Transportation, gardening, shopping services, and nearby medical care can make it easy to live without the aid of relatives. Some communities offer dining buffets every evening for residents who don't cook. The children and grandchildren can come for a visit but are not expected to care for the daily needs of their elderly relatives.

Organizational Structure: _____

2.

The trend of age-restricted living for seniors has resulted in entire communities created to suit the needs of one age group. The two contradictory needs for independence and connection are almost perfectly balanced. While the services support the independence of the elderly, the recreational facilities, clubs, groups, and classes provide an opportunity for interaction and fun with others. At the same time that elders enjoy the privacy of small homes and apartments of their own, they can take advantage of the closeness of friends. When choosing a place to live, the elderly don't need to glue themselves to relatives who can care for them. They can choose a place where they envision only their own happiness. Mary Alice asked herself, "If I were free to live anywhere, where would I want to live? Then I made myself free."

Organizational Structure: _____

Using Quotations

Earlier, you learned that an interesting quotation can provide an effective opening for an introduction. A quotation can also support the controlling idea in a body paragraph. Be careful not to overuse direct quotations. When should you quote?

- When another writer has stated something so clearly, concisely, or eloquently that you want to include his or her exact words
- When you want to include the exact words of an authority on the subject
- When you interview someone and want to include his or her spoken statement to illustrate a point
- When a quotation will add a livelier tone to the essay

In "Not Your Mother's Retirement Community," the writer includes the exact words of an authority on senior housing. The quotation emphasizes and gives more specific information for the sentence that comes before it.

> Such changes are the fruits of both good planning and good business sense. Developers have had six decades to anticipate the boomers' retirement, and they have long been plotting ways to woo them. Lately, they've been putting their plans into action. "The senior-housing business has changed dramatically over the last seven or eight years," says David Schless, president of the American Senior Housing Association.

Focused Practice

A. *Underline the quotation in the body paragraph. Then read the list of reasons on page 177. Check (✓) the reason(s) the writer included the quotation.*

> The move from north to south, or city to suburban or rural area, can separate seniors from their children and grandchildren, depriving them of the chance to see their grandchildren on a regular basis. While their families might object to this, the seniors themselves enjoy the advantage of increased independence. Until recent years, the tradition in Spain has been for retirees to live with their grown children, but 77-year-old Spaniard Fernando Feliz is certain that he doesn't want to live with his. "I don't want to be a burden to anybody . . . I know what it was like when my wife took care of her mother, and I don't want that for my children" (Fuchs). Retirement communities are designed to support the independence of the residents. Transportation, gardening, shopping services, and nearby medical care can make it easy to live without the aid of relatives. Some communities offer dining buffets every evening for residents who don't cook. The children and grandchildren can come for a visit but are not expected to care for the daily needs of their elderly relatives.

Reasons for Including the Quotation

_____ **1.** Another writer has stated something so clearly, concisely, or eloquently that this writer wanted to include his exact words.

_____ **2.** The writer wanted to include the exact words of an authority on the subject.

_____ **3.** The writer interviewed someone and wanted to include his spoken statement to illustrate a point.

_____ **4.** The quotation adds a lively tone to the essay.

B. *Write a list of questions and interview a partner about his or her present and past living situations. (Ask some general questions about preferences in living situations.) Choose some of your partner's responses to use as full-sentence quotations. For each quoted sentence, write another sentence introducing the purpose of the quotation.*

Example:

Question:	Have you ever lived in a multi-generational household? If so, what do/did you like about it?
Sentences using a quotation:	Rosa sees many advantages of living with her family and her parents-in-law. "My children are getting to know their grandparents," she said. "We never have to call a babysitter."

Questions

1. _____

_____

2. _____

_____

3. _____

_____

Sentences Using Quotations

1. _____

_____

2. _____

_____

3. _____

_____

Your Own Writing

Planning Your Body Paragraphs

A. *Review your thesis statement and ask yourself these questions.*

- Which ideas in this statement need to be explained or supported in my essay?

- How many body paragraphs will this explanation or supporting evidence require?

- What will the organizational structure of each body paragraph be?

B. *Before you begin writing your body paragraphs, complete the outline below.*

- Copy your thesis statement from page 170.

- Review the various organizational structures you have learned (see page 174).

- Select at least two organizational structures to develop and support your topic.

- Decide on the number of paragraphs best suited to your topic.

- To experiment with different kinds of structures, complete additional outlines on a separate sheet of paper.

Essay (with two structures)

Thesis Statement: _____

_____

▷ Body Paragraph 1

    ▷ Organizational Structure: _____

    ▷ Topic Sentence: _____

    _____

        ▷ Supporting Details (reasons, examples, facts, figures, quotations):

          • _____

          • _____

          • _____

▶ Body Paragraph 2

    ▶ Organizational Structure: _____

    ▶ Topic Sentence: _____

    _____

        ▶ Supporting Details:

          • _____

          • _____

          • _____

▶ Body Paragraph 3 (Optional)

    ▶ Organizational Structure: _____

    ▶ Topic Sentence: _____

    _____

        ▶ Supporting Details:

          • _____

          • _____

          • _____

C. Checking in. *Share your outline with a partner. Did your partner . . .*

- use at least two organizational structures?
- provide interesting supporting details?
- add an interesting quotation?

Based on your partner's feedback, you may want to rewrite parts of your outline.

■ THE CONCLUSION

In the concluding paragraph of an essay with multiple organizational structures, writers return to the thesis statement in order to leave the reader with a strong impression and a clear idea about the topic.

The writer may also wish to step back from the specific focus of the essay and look at the ideas in a larger context. For example, in an essay about living situations, the writer might want to step back from a focus on the implications for residents and take a look at the implications for society as a whole.

Often writers use more than one concluding strategy in the conclusion. Here are other strategies you might want to use to end your essay on living conditions:

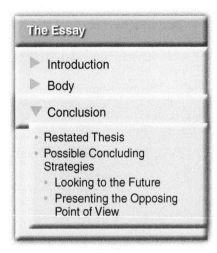

1. Look to the future of society and show how the living situation is likely to change or to change society.

2. If the issue is complex and no position is entirely right or wrong, mention the opposing point of view and its possible value.

Focused Practice

Read the following concluding paragraph and answer the questions.

> There are now 483 million people age 65 and older in the world. By the year 2030, that number is expected to grow to 974 million (O'Brien). If the trend of age-restricted living continues to grow, it could alter the social and political life of the societies where it is practiced. Will the separation of age groups rob the young of the care and wisdom of the elderly? Will the elderly lose interest in the concerns of the young, such as the quality of education? It will be interesting to see if the benefits for the elderly in forming their own communities outweigh the drawbacks for the young in losing them from our larger communities. For now, active retirement communities are a good option for retired people who value both independence and connection.

1. What is the writer's restated thesis? Circle the sentence or sentences.

2. Where does the writer discuss the implications for the society as a whole? Underline the sentences.

3. Where does the writer ask questions about the future? Check (✔) the questions you found.

4. Where does the writer mention the opposing point of view? Put an X next to the sentence.

Your Own Writing

Planning Your Conclusion

A. *What will you put in your conclusion? List your ideas here.*

_____

_____

B. *Write the sentence(s) that will remind the reader of your thesis statement.*

_____

_____

C. *What strategy will you use to close the essay?*

_____

_____

D. Checking in. *Share your ideas with a partner. Did your partner . . .*

- choose an effective concluding strategy?
- return to the idea in the thesis statement in a new and interesting way?

Writing Your First Draft

A. *Read the* Tip for Writers. *Review your graphic organizers and your notes on pages 170 and 178–179. Then write the first draft of your essay. When you are finished, give your essay a working title.*

B. *After you write the first draft, put in citations for any sources you used. Use MLA style for citations within and at the end of your essay. See Unit 2 (pages 49–50) and the Appendix on pages 194–195 for more information on MLA style.*

C. *Hand in your draft to your teacher.*

> **Tip for Writers**
>
> When you write your first draft, be sure that you maintain a reasonable tone. Your tone can, at the same time, be funny or serious, lively or slow, formal or informal.

Revising your work is an essential part of the writing process. This is your opportunity to be sure that your essay has all the important pieces and that it is clear.

Focused Practice

A. *You have read parts of this essay. Now read the entire essay to see how the parts fit together.*

Active Retirement Communities

Mary Alice Stephen loves living in Oakmont Village in Santa Rosa, California. "We have 87 interest groups, in everything from politics to yoga," she says. "And if that's not enough for you, you can start another one." Like millions of other seniors around the world, Mary Alice hopes to enjoy many years of active retirement in a community that doesn't allow anyone under the age of 55 to buy or even rent property. These active retirement communities, which offer small individual homes or apartments, recreational facilities, and services for seniors, have been criticized for removing seniors from the real world where they have spent their lives. Even worse, that real world includes the children and grandchildren with whom they could be spending their last years. However, even with these drawbacks, active retirement communities are a good choice for retired people because they offer important advantages over other options.

When people reach the end of their work lives and are no longer geographically tied to their jobs, they have the option of untying all their other knots and moving to a new community that appeals to them more. When comparing their current neighborhoods with active retirement communities, people consider many factors. It is true that the towns and cities where they have lived their whole lives have much to offer, including a diversity of age groups and their activities. Retired people enjoy having the time to volunteer in neighborhood schools, stroll in interesting shopping districts, and see their familiar neighbors. However, although many retired people would regret leaving these opportunities, they wouldn't miss many of the negative sides of their age-diverse neighborhoods. Children can be noisy, and cities can be dangerous. Most retirement communities are safe, quiet havens far from crime and pollution. Some are even far from the cold weather that many older people detest. In Europe, for example, most retirement communities are opening in warm regions, such as southern Spain, where retirees from the cold north flock like birds who have flown south for their last winters.

(continued)

The move from north to south, or city to suburban or rural area, can separate seniors from their children and grandchildren, depriving them of the chance to see their grandchildren on a regular basis. While their families might object to this, the seniors themselves enjoy the advantage of increased independence. Until recent years, the tradition in Spain has been for retirees to live with their grown children, but 77-year-old Spaniard Fernando Feliz is certain that he doesn't want to live with his. "I don't want to be a burden to anybody . . . I know what it was like when my wife took care of her mother, and I don't want that for my children" (Fuchs). Retirement communities are designed to support the independence of the residents. Transportation, gardening, shopping services, and nearby medical care can make it easy to live without the aid of relatives. Some communities offer dining buffets every evening for residents who don't cook. The children and grandchildren can come for a visit but are not expected to care for the daily needs of their elderly relatives.

The trend of age-restricted living for seniors has resulted in entire communities created to suit the needs of one age group. The two contradictory needs for independence and connection are almost perfectly balanced. While the services support the independence of the elderly, the recreational facilities, clubs, groups, and classes provide an opportunity for interaction and fun with others. At the same time that elders enjoy the privacy of small homes and apartments of their own, they can take advantage of the closeness of friends. When choosing a place to live, the elderly don't need to glue themselves to relatives who can care for them. They can choose a place where they envision only their own happiness. Mary Alice asked herself, "If I were free to live anywhere, where would I want to live? Then I made myself free."

There are now 483 million people age 65 and older in the world. By the year 2030, that number is expected to grow to 974 million (O'Brien). If the trend of age-restricted living continues to grow, it could alter the social and political life of the societies where it is practiced. Will the separation of age groups rob the young of the care and wisdom of the elderly? Will the elderly lose interest in the concerns of the young, such as the quality of education? It will be interesting to see if the benefits for the elderly in forming their own communities outweigh the drawbacks for the young in losing them from our larger communities. For now, active retirement communities are a good option for retired people who value both independence and connection.

(continued)

Works Cited

Fuchs, Dale. "In Europe, care for the elderly is being transformed." *New York Times.*
New York Times, 13 Apr. 2007. Web. 29 Apr. 2011.

O'Brien, Sharon. "Fun Facts About the Senior Population: Demographics."
About.com. The New York Times Company, 8 May 2009. Web. 18 Feb. 2011.

Stephen, Mary Alice. Personal interview. 16 Feb. 2011.

B. *Work with a partner. Answer the questions about the essay.*

1. Did the writer open the essay with an interesting quotation? If so, circle it.

2. What is the thesis statement? Underline it.

3. What parts of the thesis statement are developed in the body paragraphs? Circle them.

4. What is the controlling idea of paragraph 2? Underline the sentence that states it.

5. What is the organizational structure of paragraph 2? _____

6. Which sentence provides a transition into paragraph 3? Circle it.

7. What is the controlling idea of paragraph 3? Underline the sentence that states it.

8. What is the organizational structure of paragraph 3? _____

9. What is the controlling idea of paragraph 4? Underline the sentence that states it.

10. What is the organizational structure of paragraph 4? _____

11. What details support the controlling ideas in each body paragraph? Check (✓) the specific examples, facts, or quotations in each body paragraph.

12. Where in the concluding paragraph does the writer add numbers to show the significance of the issue? Underline the sentence(s).

13. How many people were cited by the author? _____ Circle their names.

C. **Checking in.** *Discuss your marked-up essays with another pair of students. Then in your group, share what you found most interesting about the essay. Explain your answer.*

Building Word Knowledge

The writer included several examples of figurative language in "Active Retirement Communities."

Write sentences using figurative language from the essay. The first sentence is done for you.

1. Write a sentence using **untying knots** to describe a separation.

> When people reach the end of their work lives and are no longer geographically **tied** to their jobs, they have the option of **untying all their other knots** and moving to a new community that appeals to them more.

When I moved to the United States, I had to untie all the knots that bound me to my school, my church, and my friends.

2. Write a sentence in which you call a place a **haven** (a shelter of safety or sanctuary).

> Most retirement communities are safe, quiet **havens** far from crime and pollution.

_____

_____

3. Write a sentence comparing an action of people to an action in nature.

> In Europe, for example, most retirement communities are opening in warm regions, such as southern Spain, where retirees from the cold north **flock like birds who have flown south for their last winters**.

_____

_____

(continued)

4. Write a sentence describing a strong connection as *glue*.

> When choosing a place to live, the elderly don't need to *glue* themselves to relatives who can care for them.

_____

_____

Your Own Writing

Revising Your Draft

A. *Reread the first draft of your essay. Use the Revision Checklist to identify parts of your writing that might need improvement.*

B. *Review your plans and notes, and your responses to the Revision Checklist. Then revise your first draft. Save your revised essay. You will look at it again in the next section.*

Revision Checklist

Did you . . .

☐ maintain a reasonable tone in your essay?

☐ open your essay with an interesting quotation or other opening strategy?

☐ express the controlling idea of the entire essay in your thesis statement?

☐ give enough background information in your introduction?

☐ develop the controlling idea in your thesis statement in each of your body paragraphs?

☐ use at least two organizational structures in your body paragraphs?

☐ give enough details, such as facts, figures, and quotations, to support the controlling idea of each paragraph?

☐ restate the controlling idea of the entire essay in your conclusion?

☐ use an effective concluding strategy?

☐ use figurative language in your essay?

☐ give your essay a good title?

☐ cite any sources you used in your essay?

■ GRAMMAR PRESENTATION

Before you hand in your revised essay, you must check it for any errors in grammar, punctuation, and spelling. In this section, you will learn about the subjunctive. You will focus on this grammar when you edit and proofread your essay.

The Subjunctive

Grammar Notes	Examples
1. The **subjunctive** is somewhat uncommon in English. However, one common example is the use of *were* in unreal conditions.	• If I **were** retired, I would move to a warm climate. *(I'm not retired.)* • I would stay here if it **weren't** so cold in the winter. *(It is cold in the winter.)*
Be Careful! This use of *were* occurs only in present unreal conditions. It is not used for past situations.	• If I **had been** in town, I would have helped my mother move. Not: If I ~~were~~ in town, I would have helped my mother move.
2. **Unreal conditions** with *were* are sometimes expressed by deleting *if* and **inverting** the subject and the verb. The inverted form is more formal.	• **If I were to have** children, I would want to live near my family. • **Were I to have** children, I would want to live near my family.
3. Another form of the **subjunctive** uses the **base form** of a verb in noun clauses.	main clause noun clause • My mother insists (that) she **have** her own kitchen.
Be Careful! The verb in the main clause can be past, present, or future. However, the subjunctive verb is the base form.	• We recommended (that) she **sell** her house. Not: We recommended that she ~~sold~~ her house.
Form the negative of a subjunctive verb by placing *not* before the base form.	• I suggested (that) my aunt **not move** too far away.
To form a passive subjunctive, use *be* + the past participle.	• The doctor recommends that my father **be hospitalized**.
Note: In noun clauses with subjunctive constructions, we can usually omit the word *that*.	*(continued)*

4. The **subjunctive** is used in noun clauses following **verbs of advice**, **necessity**, and **urgency**, such as *demand, insist, propose, recommend,* and *suggest.*

- I **propose** (that) we **ask** Mom and Dad to live with us.

Be Careful! We do not use infinitives after these verbs.

- The doctor **suggested** (that) she **move** to a warmer climate.
  Not: The doctor suggested ~~her to move~~.

Note: *Insist (on), propose, recommend,* and *suggest* can also be followed by a gerund phrase.

- We **insist on / propose / recommend / suggest** researching all the possibilities.

5. The **subjunctive** is also used after **adjectives of advice**, **necessity**, and **urgency**, such as *advisable, crucial, desirable, essential, important, mandatory, necessary,* and *urgent.* Subjunctive verbs after adjectives of urgency, necessity, and advice occur in the pattern *it + be* + adjective + *that* clause. We do not usually omit the word *that* in this type of clause.

- It is **important** that retired people **maintain** an active social life.
- It is **essential** that a retirement community **be** close to medical care.

Note: The pattern shown above can be replaced with *It + be* + adjective + *for* + noun or object pronoun + infinitive, which is more informal.

- It was **necessary for us to remain** in close touch with my grandparents.

Focused Practice

A. *Mr. and Mrs. García are looking for an active retirement community. Complete the sentences on their "wish list." Imagine what they might want.*

1. It is necessary _that a doctor's office be nearby_____.

2. It is mandatory _____.

3. It is essential _____.

4. It is crucial _____.

5. It will always be important _____.

Rewrite the sentences using the pattern It + be + *adjective* + for + *noun or object pronoun* + *infinitive.*

1. _It is necessary for a doctor's office to be nearby._____

2. _____

3. _____

4. _____

5. _____

B. *The Garcías have received a great deal of advice. Choose a verb from the box and complete each sentence with a noun clause in the subjunctive. Imagine what the people have advised.*

| insist (on) | propose | recommend | suggest |

1. The Garcías' daughter *proposed that they not sell the family's house* .

2. Mr. García's doctor _____ .

3. Mrs. García's sister _____ .

4. The director of the Desert Sun retirement community _____ .

Rewrite the sentences replacing the noun clause with a gerund phrase.

1. The Garcías' daughter *proposed not selling the family's house* .

2. Mr. García's doctor _____ .

3. Mrs. García's sister _____ .

4. The retirement community director _____ .

C. *The Garcías have decided not to buy a house in the Desert Sun retirement community. Read their letter. Then restate their reasons using the subjunctive in the unreal conditional.*

> Dear Director,
>
> We want to thank you for all the time you spent showing us around Desert Sun and to let you know that we will not be buying a house. There are several reasons for our decision. We are not accustomed to the desert, so we would not feel comfortable in the extreme heat. The quiet location is lovely, but there is no airport within 100 miles, so we would not be able to travel easily. We aren't young enough to use all the recreational facilities. Most importantly, the only house you have available is too small for visits from our grandchildren.
>
> Sincerely,
> Juan and Patricia García

1. *If we were accustomed to the desert, we would feel comfortable in the extreme heat.*

_____

2. _____

_____

3. _____

_____

4. _____

_____

Rewrite the unreal conditional sentences on page 189 by inverting the subject and verb.

1. _Were we accustomed to the desert, we would feel comfortable in the extreme heat._

2. _____

3. _____

4. _____

D. *Read and edit the email. There are nine mistakes in the use of the subjunctive. The first one is already corrected. Find and correct eight more. Some errors can be corrected in more than one way.*

Hi, Rosa.

    I'm really enjoying our life in Oakmont Village! I love our little house here. I
           that
insisted ~~on~~ we buy a house with a bedroom for you on your visits. From the

window of the guest room, you can see our little garden. Of course, it is essential

that us to have some help with the gardening, so I will check to see if the gardening

is provided by the Village. If I was a little younger, I would love to do the gardening

myself because the weather is usually warm enough to go outside.

    Do you remember suggesting us to join a club to meet people? What a good

idea! So far, we have joined the bridge club and the Spanish language club. We

have made some friends and learned about the area. It's important for us hosting

some of the meetings, so I'm trying to finish decorating the house.

    My only problem is with one of my neighbors. She demands me to stop

feeding the birds and wild animals. If were she friendly about it, I might be more

willing to compromise.

    Please come visit soon. I recommend fly into the nearest airport and take the

shuttle that comes right to our clubhouse.

Love,

Patricia

E. *Write five sentences related to the assignment you chose on page 164. Use the subjunctive in noun clauses and in unreal conditional sentences as in the chart on pages 187–188. These may be sentences you already have in your essay.*

1. _____

   _____

2. _____

   _____

3. _____

   _____

4. _____

   _____

5. _____

   _____

Your Own Writing

Editing Your Draft

A. *Use the Editing Checklist to edit and proofread your essay.*

B. *Prepare a clean copy of the final draft of your essay and hand it in to your teacher.*

Editing Checklist
Did you . . .
☐ use the subjunctive as necessary in noun clauses and unreal conditional sentences?
☐ use correct punctuation and spelling?
☐ use figurative language and other language correctly?

Map of the World

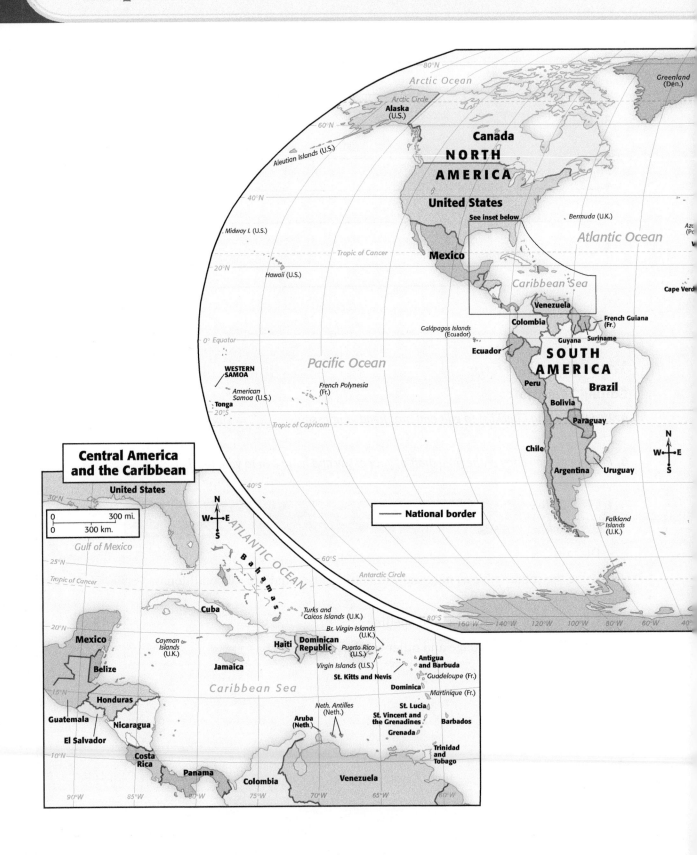

Central America and the Caribbean

National border

Appendix

■ RESEARCHING A TOPIC

Use the library and the Internet to find out more about your topic. For each source you use, record the author, title, date, publisher, and medium (e.g., print, Web, DVD).

Using Resources. The library contains a wide range of printed books, magazines, and reference materials (encyclopedias, atlases, and books of facts) that you can use to find information. Look for two or three books or articles with information about your topic. Although you can begin researching your topic in an encyclopedia, most instructors will not allow you to use this information as a cited source in your paragraph or essay. If you find information in an encyclopedia, look at the end of the entry for titles of individual books and articles about your topic; try to locate and use these sources.

One of the quickest ways to search for information is to use the Internet. Today, many books, articles, and reference books are available online. To do an online search, select keywords or a key question. Then type it into a search engine, such as Google, Yahoo, or Bing. Keep your online search as narrow as possible. Otherwise you will have to look through too many sources.

Suppose that you wanted to find out about the legally blind musher Rachael Scdoris who competed in the Iditarod in 2005. Here are some examples of specific keywords and questions that would help you find sources about her.

Examples:

Keywords:

Iditarod competitor Rachael Scdoris
Rachael Scdoris and the 2005 Iditarod

Key Questions:

Who is the Iditarod competitor Rachael Scdoris?
What happened when Rachael Scdoris competed in the 2005 Iditarod?

Evaluating Resources. Once you locate a source, think critically about it.

- When was it published? Is it up to date?
- Is it published by a well-known and reliable place (e.g., a mainstream newspaper or government website)?
- Does it present a balanced and unbiased point of view, or is it only expressing one person's opinion?
- Does it contain facts that can be double-checked in another source?

Evaluate each source you use, especially, the sources you find on the Internet. Some Internet sites contain inaccurate information, so limit your sources to trusted sites.

■ CITING SOURCES IN YOUR WRITING

When you are writing a paragraph or essay, always acknowledge your sources of information or any wording that is not your own. If you do not cite your sources, including the words, ideas, or research that you have borrowed from others, you are *plagiarizing*, or stealing other people's ideas. This is a serious offense that is treated very severely in an academic environment.

In colleges and universities, one of the most commonly used styles for handling citations is the MLA (Modern Language Association) style. According to the MLA style, you cite your sources in two places: within the text and in a "Works Cited" list.*

In-Text Citations. Most of the wording in your paragraphs and essays should be your own. When you paraphrase or quote what other people have said or researched, give a brief citation for the source in parentheses at the end of the sentence. If you have already mentioned the author within the sentence, you do not need to repeat the name at the end.

Examples:

Citing a Fact: According to a 2011 report, Twitter has only 21 million active users (Bennett).

Citing a Paraphrase: The legendary journalist spoke of the need to support public broadcasting (Moyers). [or] Bill Moyers, a legendary journalist, spoke of the need to support public broadcasting.

Citing a Quote: On her website, the legally blind musher says: "I hope my story can help encourage others to pursue their dreams" (Scdoris).

A List of Works Cited. At the end of your writing, provide a list of all the sources you have cited. Type "Works Cited" at the top of the list and center the heading. Then organize your sources alphabetically according to the author's last name. If the source has no author, alphabetize it according to its title. Indent the second line of the source.

The basic format for individual citations and a "Works Cited" list is shown in the examples below.

Examples:

For Articles: Author. "Article Title." *Magazine Title* date: page no. medium.

For Books: Author. *Book Title*. publisher, date: page no. medium.

For Personal Interviews: Name of Interviewee. Personal interview. date.

For Websites: Website title. publisher, date. medium. date accessed. <URL>

Works Cited

Collum, Danny Duncan. "How to save journalism: can a government-subsidized press save democracy?" *Sojourners* June 2009: 40. Print.

Miller, Claire Cain. "The New News Junkie Is Online and On the Phone." *New York Times* 1 Mar. 2010. Print.

Noone, Joan. Personal interview. 20 July 2011.

---

* The format for citing other sources can also be found in MLA handbooks, on the websites for most college and university libraries in North America, or by searching the Internet using the keywords *MLA style*. For electronic sources, MLA style no longer requires writers to include web addresses, or URLs, but some instructors may still require them. Some instructors will also allow you to use citation generators that are available online. Check with your teacher about his or her requirements.

Index

Acknowledgments

I would like to thank my students at City College of San Francisco for their willingness to work with new materials and do their best. I am especially grateful to Mengci Chen and Wei Wang for contributing their writing. I would like to thank Mary Alice Stephen for her interview in Oakmont Village and my husband, Charlie Stephen, for his invaluable assistance and support.

Laura Walsh

Credits